EXPLORING EGYPT

D0878364

Horus
'Lord of the Sky'
God of Kingship
Son of Osiris & Isis

EXPLORING EGYPT

A Traveler's View of an Ancient Civilization

Dick Lutz

Photographs by Mary Lutz

DIMI PRESS   Salem, Oregon

© 2007 by Dick Lutz

DIMI PRESS
3820 Oak Hollow Lane SE
Salem, Oregon 97302

ISBN (10 digit) :0-931625-44-0
ISBN (13 digit) :978- 0-931625-44-2

Library of Congress Control Number: 2007901073

Cover design by Bruce DeRoos

Cover photos by Ralph Hammelbacher

Dedicated to all travelers everywhere.

May they promote peace in the world.

Hathor
'Lady of the Universe'
Great Cow/Sky Goddess

ACKNOWLEDGEMENTS

In addition to the works listed in the Bibliography, I wish to thank the following individuals for assistance in reviewing the manuscript: Ralph Hammelbacher, President and Charlie Boyd, Art Director, of International Expeditions. Also Morgen Lutzross reviewed the manuscript.

The excellent editing of the book was done by Janis Hunt Johnson of Ask Janis.

Research for EXPLORING EGYPT was done primarily in two libraries: Salem, Oregon Public Library and the Mark Hatfield Library of Willamette University. Dick Ferrell provided a number of books for research from his private collection.

I also owe a debt of gratitude to Karima, our guide, for an excellent introduction to the grandeur, that was and is, Egypt.

In addition to the photographs by Mary Lutz, the use of the photos of Douglas Bartlett, Ralph Hammelbacher, and Vladimir Pomort- zeff is appreciated.

Maat
Goddess of
Cosmic Harmony
Truth, Justice
& Order

INTRODUCTION

It is difficult to encapsulate all that is known about ancient Egypt in one book. Therefore, I have given in Part I an overview of the 5,000-year history of ancient Egypt including some specific examples of the pharaohs and the gods they worshipped. Also information about some of the interesting aspects of ancient Egyptian life. Part II covers the 2300 years between ancient or pharaonic Egypt and the current period. Part III is a description of my tour of ancient Egyptian sites as well as information about those sites. Part IV is a description of the situation in modern Egypt, including Cairo.

For more information on any specific subject touched upon in the book, see the Annotated Bibliography. I have endeavored to describe each reference in such detail that the interested person can easily obtain more complete information on the subject of his/her interest.

Amazon.com lists over 9,000 books about Egypt so I certainly haven't researched them all but I think I've done a pretty good job of using the best.

A confusing fact (at least to me) is that Upper Egypt and the Upper Nile are down south near Sudan. It seems that anything that is south should be called

Lower rather than Upper. The explanation is simple — the Nile River is one of the few north-flowing rivers in the world. Since upper means near the origin of the river in this case it is the southern part.

Almost all travelers to Egypt purchase mementoes of their experience. Since Egypt is a poor country and tourism is such a significant part of their economy, it follows that their are lots of people offering to sell things. Sometimes these vendors get in your face and may be annoying. Rather than get angry I advise reminding your self that these salesmen (the're seldom women) are simply trying to eke out a living. Be patient with them and you will enjoy your visit more.

All photos not otherwise attributed are the work of Mary Lutz.

Osiris
God of
the Dead

PREVIOUS BOOKS BY DICK LUTZ

Feel Better! Live Longer! Relax!

The Running Indians

Komodo: The Living Dragon (co-authored with J. Marie Lutz)

Hidden Amazon

Patagonia: At the Bottom of the World

Belize: Reefs, Rain Forests, and Mayan Ruins

Tuatara: A Living Fossil

CONTENTS

Sphinx and Khafre's Pyramid

PART I

ANCIENT EGYPT

Isis
'Great of Magic'
Sister-Wife
of Osiris

BEGINNING

The imposing monuments of ancient Egypt have fascinated the entire world for thousands of years. The first recorded tourist visit took place over 2,500 years ago, but travelers probably came before that. The pyramids at Giza and the Sphinx may be the most well known of the many attractions left by the ancient Egyptians, but there is much more to be learned about this civilization and its culture.

As the world's first nation-state it was basically a theocracy. There was no concept of separation of church and state. Kings were very close to being considered gods themselves. People started to call the kings pharaohs sometime between 1554 and 1304 BC. "Pharaoh" means "big house" in Egyptian.

The chronology of ancient Egypt is only an estimate. Generally speaking, the dates after about 500 BC can be considered accurate. Between 1500 BC and 500 BC a margin of error of 50 years is appropriate, while a 100-year margin of error is best used before 1500 BC.

HISTORY

The first humans to come into the Nile valley arrived thousands of years ago. By 5000 BC the hunters had become farmers and the first settlements appeared. However, the first written texts discovered date is from 2950 BC. This can be considered approximately the date of the beginning of the civilization known as ancient Egypt.

It was about 3000 BC that the warrior Menes is supposed to have marched his army northwards along the Nile conquering the independent clusters of people, and eventually crowning himself king of Upper and Lower Egypt. This is one version of the story of the first king.

As we will see many times in this book, Egyptologists disagree about the accuracy of this account. One of the problems is that the Egyptian meaning of the name Menes is *meni* which also means "so and so." Menes may or may not have actually lived. One scientist refers to him as a King Arthur–like personage.

There were many pharaohs over the twenty-seven (or more) centuries of pharaonic Egypt. Here is a timeline of some of the most famous developments in ancient Egypt

2950 BC — Earliest texts (found at Abydos).

2630 BC — Step pyramid constructed at Sakkara.

2550 BC — Great Pyramid of Khufu.

1493 BC — Valley of the Kings founded.

1353 BC — The reign of Akhenaten began, marking the beginning of the Amarna period.

1111 BC — Major investigation of tomb robbery at the Valley of the Kings was under way.

525 BC — Egypt conquered by the Persians.

332 BC — Egypt conquered by Alexander, ending pharaonic rule in Egypt.

RELIGION AND THE AFTERLIFE

A superficial look at ancient Egypt leaves one with the impression that the ancient Egyptians were obsessed with death. But a closer analysis demonstrates that the truth is a little more complicated than that. The ancient Egyptians worshipped many gods, but always the focus of their religious beliefs was on the afterlife. Death was simply a passage between this life and the afterlife. It has been said that the Egyptians loved life so much that they planned to live after death.

The king (or pharaoh) was considered to be semi-divine and as such was basically worshipped by the people. There were many elaborate rituals, some only performed by the king. These rituals, which we would call religious in nature, were held at specified intervals for the purpose of glorifying the gods. (If this isn't religion, I don't know what is).

Of course, as with so many aspects of their culture, the details changed over time. The most dramatic change came during the reign of Akhenaten (1353 – 1336 BC.) After assuming the job of Pharaoh he changed his name from Amenhotep IV, built a new capital, and declared Egypt a monotheistic state. His seventeen-year rule was disastrous for the economy and for Egypt in general.

Not a great deal is known about the religious beliefs of the common people, as almost all of the recorded texts and artistic productions depict royalty (sometimes with their servants). The ordinary people were not allowed in the great temples, but they had their own centers of worship. These were either small shrines or household shrines at which they worshipped their own favorite god(s.) The choice of god(s) might be related to their occupation. For instance, a scribe might choose the god Thoth, the inventor of numbers and the patron of writing. Or the great gods such as Hathor or Osiris might be chosen.

Two of the most popular household gods were quite bizarre-looking. Tawaret was a hippopotamus goddess and the protector of women in childbirth. Bes looked like a deformed monster but was viewed as jolly and in charge of fun and games. He is the only Egyptian god who is regularly depicted from the front. His grotesque figure frequently appeared in bedrooms.

EGYPT AND THE BIBLE

Not a single bit of evidence exists in Egypt that supports the Bible narratives. Yet Egypt is mentioned hundreds of times in the Bible and there are many Old Testament stories concerning Egypt.

There are two theories for this lack of reference in Egyptian history to biblical events. One theory is that the people who can be compared to the figures of the Old Testament did indeed live. It is not surprising that their names and deeds have not survived.

The second theory holds that the stories of the Old Testament are great literature but not actual history. This theory is backed up by the observation that the stories mention Egypt in only general terms; kings are simply "pharaoh" with no name given. Also, descriptions of the geography and government of Egypt are vague and the major events of Egyptian history are not mentioned.

PHARAOHS

The mission of the pharaoh was basically to retain *maat* or order. Because of the pharaoh's semi-divine status he/she could get thousands of skilled workers to build huge projects (the Great Pyramid is perhaps the most outstanding example). These projects were usually either tombs or temples, and were almost invariably dedicated solely to the glory of the pharaoh.. One of the pharaohs (Pepi II) reigned for 97 years. He is believed to be the longest ruling national leader in the history of the world.

Rather than try to describe the reign of each pharaoh let's look at just a few.

DJOSER — He is the best-known pharaoh of the Third dynasty of Egypt. His claim to fame is that he commissioned Imhotep to build the Step Pyramid at Sakkara. (See below for more on Imhotep.)

The statue of Djoser in the Egyptian Museum in Cairo is the oldest known Egyptian life-size statue. It was found at Sakkara and a plaster replica of the statue is kept there.

Djoser ruled for nineteen years (2668 – 2649 BC). Although there is some dispute among Egyptologists, he probably was the first king of the Third Dynasty. Although little is known about the reign of Djoser, one fact that is known is that he sent his military into the Sinai Peninsula and subdued the local inhabitants. It is also known that he sent expeditions to the Sinai to mine for turquoise and copper. It is believed that the southern boundary of his kingdom was at the First Cataract, which is near Aswan.

Archeologists have found indications that Djoser commissioned construction projects in cities other than Sakkara. There is an inscription that claims that it was created during the reign of Djoser but it has been determined that it actually was done during the Ptolemaic Dynasty some 2,000 years later. This inscription describes how Djoser ended a seven-year famine by rebuilding the temple of the god Khnum on the island of Elephantine. Some Egyptologists consider this story as simply a legend.

Imhotep was the first architect and physician known by name in written history. He has been called Egypt's Leonardo but he probably was even more versatile than the Italian. Imhotep designed, and supervised the construction of, the step pyramid at Sakkara. This was the first pyramid built in Egypt and its construction proved that pyramids could be built. He may also have been the first to use columns in architecture. But being the first architect and building the first pyramid was not enough.

Imhotep, whose name means "the one who comes in peace," was also the founder of Egyptian medicine. Among other abilities he had a reputation for helping women to conceive. He was considered a genius, and two thousand years after his death his status was raised to that of a god.

There is a theory that Imhotep is similar to the biblical Joseph. It has been suggested that the Joseph of the Bible is a composite of a Hebrew individual and Imhotep. (There is much conjecture in Egyptology.)

KHUFU (also known as Cheops) — He was a Pharaoh of ancient Egypt's Old Kingdom. It was thought he reigned from around 2589 – 2566 BC. But recent radiocarbon dating puts his reign around 2694 BC. Khufu was the second pharaoh of the Fourth Dynasty. He is the builder of the Great Pyramid of Giza, the only one of the Seven Wonders of the Ancient World still standing.

Folklore claims that Khufu was a cruel and ruthless pharaoh. Khufu had several sons, one of which, Djedefra, was his immediate successor. For some reason Khufu's second son, Khafre, took over the throne and built the other huge pyramid at Giza. Khufu also had a daughter named Queen Hetepheres II.

Indications are that Khufu led military expeditions to the Sinai, Nubia, and Libya. A papyrus written long after Khufu's death describes him being told magical tales by his sons, Khafre and Djedefra. It is this document that depicts Khufu as mean and cruel, but whether this is the truth or not remains unclear.

Khufu's mummy has never been found although an empty sarcophagus is located in the King's Chamber inside the Great Pyramid. Ironically, the only representation of this Pharaoh who built the largest building in the ancient world is a miniature statuette that is only 3 in (7.6 cm) in height. This tiny statue is lodged in the Egyptian Antiquities Museum in Cairo.

Khufu was the first of the pyramid builders to construct several minor pyramids around his large one. It is believed that these were intended for members of his royal household.

MENTUHOTEP II — . He was a successful pharaoh who ruled from 2061 – 2010 BC. Prior to his reign Egypt had become divided, but he reunited the nation and made Egypt prosperous once more.

Following the reunification of his country, Mentuhotep campaigned along the Mediterranean coast in both directions thus expanding the territory controlled by Egypt. Upon his death he left a united and wealthy nation.

HATSHEPSUT — She reigned from c.1503 – 1482 BC, the fifth pharaoh of the Eighteenth Dynasty of ancient Egypt. Hatshepsut is one of the best known of the several queens that ruled in ancient Egypt. She is also considered to be one of the most successful pharaohs, commissioning hundreds of construction projects and rebuilding Egypt's trade networks. Hatshepsut is often regarded as the first great woman in recorded history.

She was the wife of Thutmose II and, following his death, became the interregnum regent for Thutmo se III who was still a child. Hatshepsut was evidently both the boy king's aunt and stepmother. Before the boy achieved maturity, Hatshepsut usurped the throne and had herself crowned Pharaoh.

She was the first to import foreign trees, having thirty-one frankincense trees planted in the courts of her mortuary temple. These trees had been brought back to Egypt by a military expedition to Punt (in present-day Somalia).

So much statuary were produced during her reign that museum collections of them exist around the world. The Metropolitan Museum of Art in New York had a Hatshepsut exhibit in 2006.

Among her many building projects is her own mortuary temple at Deir el-Bahri. This colonnaded structure, designed in perfect symmetry, predates the Greek Parthenon by nearly a thousand years. Hatshepsut also had built a number of obelisks including the Unfinished Obelisk at Aswan.

Since at this period pharaoh was an exclusively male title and there was no word for a regnant queen, only for a queen consort, Hatshepsut took the title of king.

She assumed the regalia and symbols of the pharaonic office including the false beard. Some depictions of Hatshepsut even omit her breasts. After becoming king, she changed her name from the feminine Hatshepsut to the masculine Hatshepsu.

There is some indication that Hatshepsut had a male advisor (and perhaps lover) named Senenmut. Evidently the kings had the right to have sexual relations with whomever they wished, so why not this female king?

AKHENATEN — He ruled from c.1353-1336 BC and was also known as Amenhotep IV. He was a religious revolutionary, raising the obscure god Aten to the position of supreme being. For thousands of years the Egyptians had worshipped dozens of gods but Akhenaten introduced monotheism.

Aten was the name for the sun. Akhenaten proclaimed the visible sun itself the supreme deity. However, only the royal family was permitted to interact with, and perform rituals for, Aten. Like many of the pharaohs, Akhenaten built massive temple complexes, including one at Karnak. His temples provided for worship in the open sunlight, rather than in dark enclosures.

As many pharaohs before and after him had done, Akhenaten had many of his predecessors' representations defaced. He went beyond the others by having religious symbols also defaced. He even ordered the destruction of the temples of Amun, the central figure of the previous religion. Akhenaten seems to have neglected matters of state resulting in some disorder in various parts of the Egyptian empire. There is even some indication that he was partially responsible for the spread of a pandemic during his reign.

The Amarna period is the term given to Akhenaten's reign. The period is considered by most Egyptologists to be one of change and discord. Following Akhenaten's death the Egyptian panoply of gods returned to popular favor and almost all mention of Akhenaten's name was eradicated. The city he founded, Akhetaten, was abandoned and eventually fell into ruin.

Akhenaten is the most controversial pharaoh in ancient Egyptian history. He has been compared at various times to modern figures running the gamut from Martin Luther to Hitler, and from Anwar Sadat, to Jesus Christ.

Nefertiti was the chief wife of Akhenaten and bore him six daughters and a son. Nefertiti's name is known, at least in the West, primarily because of the beautiful bust of her that has survived.

Reproductions of that bust are one of the most common symbols of Ancient Egypt.

The power and respect held by Nefertiti was unusual for a queen. There is reason to believe that she was named co-regent with her husband Akhenaten during the last years of his reign.

TUTANKHAMEN —The boy who ruled from 1333 – 1324 BC is possibly the best known of Egypt's pharaohs. This is because his tomb revealed an abundance of fantastically beautiful objects, including the golden mask that is a signature of ancient Egypt.

Actually, his rule as pharaoh was unremarkable. He was the son of Akhenaten and Nefertiti. Or he might have had another mother. His original name was Tutankhaten "living image of Aten" but after his father's death he changed it to Tutankhamen "living image of Amun." This change indicated that he rejected his father's religion and returned to that of old.

Tutankhamen — the boy we call King Tut — began his reign at age nine, married his half-sister, and died in his teens. There has been much speculation on the cause of his death, including the suspicion that he was murdered. But a 2005 examination of his mummy, including a CT scan, determined that he died of gangrene poisoning after breaking his leg.

The discovery of Tutankhamen's tomb and its fabulous contents by Howard Carter in 1922 resulted in renewed interest in all things Egyptian.

RAMSES II – This pharaoh was also known as Ramses the Great. He ruled from 1304 – 1237 BC or 1279 – 1213 BC, depending on which Egyptologist you read. He was one of twelve pharaohs named Ramses but he was the longest ruling and, as far as we know, accomplished more than any of the others of the same name.

A warrior-king, Ramses II led his troops in several campaigns. One of his wars ended with the earliest known peace treaty in the world. He constructed many impressive monuments and statues. He built Abu Simbel and the mortuary temple at Luxor known as the Ramesseum.
\
It is believed by some scholars that Ramses II was the pharaoh of Exodus. A huge (83-ton) statue of Ramses II exists in Cairo. In August 2006 this statue was moved from near the Cairo train station, where it was deteriorating due to pollution, to a site not far from the Giza Pyramids. The move, which took place from 1 AM to 10 AM, was watched by five million Egyptians! Ramses II's mummy is one of several mummies in the Egyptian Antiquities Museum in Cairo.

GODS

The ancient Egyptians had hundreds of gods. Here's a discussion of several of the major ones.

RA was the god of the sun and the creator of everything, including the other gods. The Egyptians, at all periods, worshipped the sun. They knew that the sun was a fire, but the idea that the blazing sun rose daily from a body of water was hard to swallow. Therefore, they came up with the idea that the sun traveled in a boat. Actually they believed that two boats were involved; the morning boat and the evening boat.

The god Ra was frequently depicted with the body of a man and the head of a hawk. The first rising of the sun was considered to be the beginning of time. There were different versions of what he is supposed to have done. For example, he was thought to pass through the underworld at night, and another belief was that he changed his boat every hour during the day and night.

As Ra was known as "father of the gods" there was also a "mother of the gods." She was known as Rat and described as "lady of heaven," "mistress of the gods," and "mistress of Heliopolis." (Today, a rather affluent neighborhood of Cairo is called Heliopolis.) As early as 3350 BC, the priests of Ra were quite powerful. The early kings of Egypt believed themselves to be the sons of Ra, the sun god.

Later, this god became known as Amun-Ra. Even later Ra became subsumed into Horus.

HORUS was a god worshipped later in the thousands of years of ancient Egypt. There are many accounts of his origin and purpose. According to one belief, he was the son of Ra, but there are many other stories about him. Like Ra, Horus was associated with the sun and is frequently depicted with the body of a man (or sometimes a lion) and the head of a hawk (or a sun). Horus was not really a replacement for Ra but rather could be considered his assistant or associate. You will see many representations of Horus as you visit the temples and tombs of ancient Egypt.

The Eye of Horus was an important symbol of power. Horus was considered the god of the sky and one account maintains he was the son of Osiris and Isis.

OSIRIS was the god of death, life, and fertility. One description of him alludes to the fact that he once possessed human form and lived on earth but was able somehow to live a new life after his death in a region where he ruled as king. Considering the importance of the afterlife to the ancient Egyptians, it is not surprising that Osiris was a major god.

The cult of Osiris existed from the earliest days of pharaonic Egypt. One of its sacraments involved eating the body (in the form of bread) and drinking the blood (ale) of the god. This sounds like the Christian sacrament of communion. Osiris was considered to be the merciful judge of the dead in the afterlife. After around 2000 BC, all people (not just pharaohs) were believed to be judged by Osiris at their death.

Osiris worship died in the sixth century AD. Its last existence took place on the Island of Philae at which time the Romans destroyed its temples.

ISIS was the wife of Osiris (and perhaps his sister) and the mother of Horus. She was considered to have magical powers and so became the goddess of magic. It has been argued that Isis worship has influenced the Christian religion as far as the veneration of the Virgin Mary is concerned.Her cult became very popular and was eventually banned by the Christians in the sixth century AD. However, it still remains today at various places around the world. In the United States it is associated with feminism.There exists an International Fellowship of Isis with headquarters in a castle in Ireland.

SETH was the god of the underworld and, like Satan, considered the evil one. He was also known as the god of disruption. There are many legends about the gods and their interaction, but perhaps the most bizarre tells of a fight between Osiris and Seth. Seth won, and dismembered the body of Osiris, and threw the parts into the Nile. Isis recovered the body parts except for the phallus that had been eaten by a fish. Isis manufactured a substitute phallus, attached it to his reassembled body and somehow this brought Osiris back to life. She then turned herself into a bird and mated with her husband. Horus was the result. (Or something like that, it's really not a very logical story).

THE NILE RIVER

It is said that Egypt would not exist but for the Nile. This famous river has been, for thousands of years, the fertilizer of the soil, the main avenue for transportation, and the giver of life. Of course, although it is still the chief road for transportation, it is no longer the enricher of the land. The building of the Aswan High Dam and the creation of Lake Nasser have changed Egypt drastically.

The Valley of the Nile is about 600 miles long (almost 1,000 kilometers) and only 10 miles wide (16 kilometers.) It constitutes about four percent of the land, yet ninety-five percent of Egyptians live there. The Nile River is the longest river in the world (although some claim the Amazon of South America is longer.) It is 4,160 mi (6,695 km) in total length. It has two main tributaries, the White Nile and the Blue Nile. The White Nile rises in the country of

Rwanda and flows through Tanzania, Uganda, and into Sudan where it joins with the Blue Nile coming from Ethiopia.

Before the construction of the Aswan High Dam the Nile flooded annually. The flooding took place from July to September as the result of the tropical rains on the Ethiopian tableland. The river normally reached its highest level in October; it then dropped to its lowest point sometime between April and June.

Red land/Black land is the expression used to describe the desert (red land) and the Nile Valley (black land.) At most parts of the Nile, the sandy desert abuts the fertile Valley of the Nile. This presents a striking picture of contrasts.

Photo by Douglas Bartlett

**Osiris
God of
the Dead**

FUNERAL PRACTICES

Burial around 5000 BC, at least by one tribe, was almost casual. There were no cemeteries or tombs. Bodies, in a contracted position, were buried in shallow graves either next to, or in, their homes. Nothing appears to have been placed with the bodies. Other groups from that early period seem to have had equally simple burial practices.

In about 3500 BC burials began to change. The graves became more elaborate with definite distinctions between rich and poor. More and more objects were buried with the dead.

Around 3000 BC Egypt began to be unified, and this is when belief in an afterlife seems to have arisen. Tombs from this period are not only larger and more ornate, but the objects interred with the deceased are things the person would presumably need in an afterlife, such as food, jewelry, and cosmetics.

Increasingly, a distinction by class is found. Tombs constructed in about 2770 BC began to be above ground in what is called a *mastaba*, or low-lying, massive mud brick structure with sloping sides, and a flat roof. It was around this time that the idea of a tomb being a house for the afterlife arose.

The first pyramid, called the Step Pyramid, was built in 2630 BC. It was built specifically as the tomb for King Djoser. It was part of a vast complex with underground rooms containing tens of thousands of stone vessels. There are three and a half miles of tunnels under the Step Pyramid.

In 2500 BC (or thereabouts) the pyramids at Giza were built. Bodies were buried in stone sarcophagi and many objects were interred with them. Many of the tombs of this period contain wall decorations, both reliefs and paintings. These decorations depict scenes from daily life as well as views of the afterlife, often in symbolic form. Sometimes ships or models of ships were buried near the tomb, such as the solar ship buried next to the Great Pyramid.

Virtually all Egyptian tombs were eventually heavily looted. Those preparing the tombs probably expected this. Thus there was a trend toward decorations representing the necessary objects accompanying the dead. It was harder to loot decorations than the objects themselves. Around 2300 BC there were more decorated coffins in place of the plain ones of earlier times. During subsequent centuries a greater variety of burial practices occurred.

For instance, the process of mummification was perfected at about this same time. It is possible that it began after it was observed that bodies buried in the dry sand of the Egyptian desert were preserved for some time. Apparently the purpose of mummification was to preserve as much of the body as possible so that the deceased could survive for a long time in the afterlife. It was believed that a person could continue to live in the afterlife if the remains of the body continued to exist.

Not only humans, but also animals were mummified. Actually, there were many more animals mummified than people. Cats, in particular, were considered to be special by the ancient Egyptians.

Mummification was the practice of preserving bodies in the following manner. The intestines, lungs, liver, and stomach were first removed. They were placed in special jars called canopic jars. These containers were frequently buried nearby the remaining body. In the more deluxe ceremonies the brain was also removed but discarded.

After removal of the entrails (perhaps because they would decay rapidly) the body was then dehydrated in natron for some forty days. Natron is a salt found in the Nile delta. The cadaver was then wrapped in linen bandages and the linen was treated with gum. Sometimes a plaster was used in place of linen.

After the body was placed in a coffin a mask was frequently placed on the coffin. The mask was an idealized version of the face of the departed. The most famous funeral mask is the golden one of King Tutankhamen.

This elaborate process was used only on royalty and, perhaps, other nobles.

PAINTING

Has there ever existed a civilization in which art was more important than that of ancient Egypt? For the ancient Egyptians art was a method of communication. Their very written language, hieroglyphics, grew out of their artistic attempts to convey the looks of things. Their early pictograms evolved into hieroglyphics. Ancient Egyptian art was not "creative." It was designed to communicate, to tell a story.

When a two-dimensional representation of a person was produced the head, trunk, and legs were shown in profile. The rest of the body was in direct frontal view. This was done to present each part of the body at its best — its most accurate. The head was shown in profile to tell the viewer more about the nature of the face than the frontal image could. However, the eye was shown in frontal view because then it was possible to portray the white of the eye, the iris, and the pupil. The shoulders were shown full frontally because that was most characteristic. The rest of the body was in profile although the chest and stomach were twisted. With the figure of a woman, the profile of a breast was usually shown. This conformed to what might be called the "code" of conveying the maximum amount of information, in this case the fact that the figure was female.

One of the purposes of Egyptian art was to guarantee the immortality of the body .Therefore the body had to be rendered exactly. Egyptian art was intellectual, not emotional. Both the sculptor and the artist used a grid, consisting of eighteen squares. This was the case for about the first 2,000 years of the Egyptian civilization. Art changed very little during this period.

Non-human objects were also shown to display their detailed real characteristics, not exactly as they really looked. Thus, a table might be shown with its legs and its top, not in perspective but with all its features revealed. A pool would be shown from above because this was thought to reveal its true characteristics while the trees surrounding it would be shown lying down. The manner in which human figures were portrayed applied primarily to pharaohs and other royalty. Workmen and lower-class figures were usually shown in total profile or even with their backs turned.

With sculpture the human form could be portrayed only with fixed axes. The sculpted figure could bend forwards or backwards but never sideways. Nor could it twist. Photographs of Egyptian sculptures are frequently taken from an angle, thus distorting the image. In a way this violates the effect for which the sculptor was striving. It takes the image out of the code in which it was created.

Size was used to show power or authority. Thus the pharaoh was almost always the largest figure in a group and his chief wife would be either the same size or smaller. Secondary wives and servants were smaller still.

In a similar manner, the lower the status of an individual in society, such as children and animals, the more freely they could be portrayed. The images of animals and birds are some of the most delightful in Egyptian art. Servants might be shown wrestling or dancing, for example, but never pharaohs.

The goal of all art was to achieve *maat*, or order. The importance of order in Egyptian culture cannot be overemphasized.

Art of the Amarna Period (around 1350 BC) was different from what had gone before. Rather than dealing with subjects such as the netherworld and resurrection, it dealt mainly with more natural topics. It focused on everyday activities such as eating, and less on the gods and the afterworld. There are even scenes of the royal family playing with their children. There is a relaxation of the formal, rigid style that had been the rule.

A peculiarity of the art of the Amarna Period was that the human figures, including the pharaoh, were portrayed as deformed. It has been speculated that Akhenaten was himself deformed in some way.

This was the period of the rule of Akhenaten who first decreed the idea of only one god, Aten, rather than the pantheon of gods that had been worshipped in prior times. Although the worship of Aten was later suppressed, the art continued to have an impact.

RELIEFS

Three techniques were used for relief sculpture. First, there were the bas-reliefs or raised reliefs. Second were the sunken reliefs carved out of the stone. This technique is also known as intaglio. In effect, this is a negative image. A third technique involved incision, or cutting into the stone.

MUSIC

An important instrument in ancient Egypt was the harp. The reliefs show several different types, from small portable ones to some taller than the person playing it. Also used were small drums and tambourines. Later, the instruments included the lyre, the oboe, and the lute. These latter three may have been imported from Asia.

THE MAKING OF PAPYRUS

The papyrus plant used to grow wild and profusely in the swampy parts of the Nile valley. It no longer is found in the wild in Egypt, but it is carefully grown in certain places, for instance outside the Cairo Museum. It is a pretty plant of tall stalks with a feathery tuft on top.

The making of papyrus — the ancient Egyptians' paper — from the papyrus plant is described thusly: A fresh papyrus plant is cut just above water level. It is then cut into lengths and the outer rind stripped off. The inner pith remaining is cut into narrow strips. The strips are then placed on an absorbent material and a second layer of strips placed on top and at right angles to the bottom layer. The strips are then pounded with a wooden mallet and subsequently placed in a press for a period of time. The juices of the papyrus serve as glue and fasten the strips together. Papyrus was normally made into scrolls rather than used in individual sheets.

LANGUAGES

There were two written languages in ancient Egypt. Hieroglyphs were used as the formal language, based on pictograms. The hieratic language developed from hieroglyphs. This was a cursive form of handwriting that apparently was much easier to use. Both were written languages; the spoken language was probably a combination of the two. (Since the ancient Egyptians left no recordings, we're not sure about this).

Over the centuries the language changed until a separate language, known as "demotic," emerged. This occurred about 650 BC. Another language was the "coptic" language, which was adopted particularly by the Christian Copts, in the fourth century AD. Later, in the seventh century AD, the Arabic language and its writing system were introduced into Egypt.

CHAMPOLLION AND THE ROSETTA STONE

In 1799, during Napoleon's foray into Egypt, a group of French soldiers were demolishing a wall in preparation for strengthening the defenses around a fort. One of the soldiers uncovered a dark grey stone slab with inscriptions on one side. This took place near the town of Rosetta. Upon examination, the Rosetta Stone was found to contain inscriptions in three different languages. One set of inscriptions was obviously Greek and could easily be translated. It proved to be a decree dated in March 196 BC. The decree was written in commemoration of the Roman reign of Ptolemy V, who ruled Egypt from 204 BC to 180 BC. The French scientists who had accompanied Napoleon to Egypt assumed that the other two languages carried the identical text and thus could be easily translated.

This proved not to be the case and it took years of hard work before the other two sets of inscriptions were understood. One was in hieroglyphics and its deciphering "cracked the code" of the ancient Egyptian language and enabled Egyptologists to eventually understand a great deal about ancient Egypt. The third language turned out to be demotic.

As Napoleon himself had virtually abandoned Egypt to return to France, his general in Egypt began negotiations with the nearby British Commander. They signed a treaty, which allowed the French to return to France with everything they had collected in Egypt. When news of the treaty reached London the British government rejected it. After a year and a half the French scientists were allowed to leave with some, but not all, of their collected items. Some of the findings, including the Rosetta Stone, were taken to England. The Rosetta Stone rests today in the British Museum.

After discovery of the Rosetta Stone, and even before it landed in England, European scientists began trying to decipher the hieroglyphics. It proved to be a very difficult task. Several books and scientific articles were published that turned out to have the wrong translation. Finally, a Frenchman by the name of Jean-Francois Champollion succeeded in figuring out the language of the hieroglyphics.

Champollion is considered the father of Egyptology as he subsequently spent years as a researcher in Egypt. He was brilliant and absolutely obsessed with the Egyptian hieroglyphics. As so often happens with scientific breakthroughs, many scientists were working on the same problem. They competed, sometimes bitterly, in trying to solve the problem.

The chief competitor to Champollion was a British physician by the name of Thomas Young. Apparently a skilled physician, he became interested in hieroglyphics as a hobby but became virtually as obsessed as Champollion. The two cooperated at first but eventually became bitter rivals.

A bust of Champollion is found in the Egyptian Museum, which provides an indication of how important his work is to an understanding of Ancient Egypt. If he, or someone else, had not translated the hieroglyphics most of the thousands of books that have been written about ancient Egypt could not have been written.

RELATIONSHIPS

It is known that brother-sister incest occurred and even brother-sister marriages took place within the royal families. An example is King Tutankhamen who is believed to have married his sister. At least one pharaoh married his own daughter. These incestuous marriages apparently took place in an attempt to preserve the royal line. There is no indication of incest in non-royal families.

Some of the pharaohs had a chief wife and secondary wives. Some experts believe that sexual intercourse with servants was a common practice. The ancient Egyptians apparently had no concept of illegitimacy or virginity.

Actually, little is known about the relationships among the royalty of the ancient Egyptians due to the formal nature of both the writings and the artwork. The focus of both was on the afterlife, not on the current life. Yet many Egyptologists believe that there are many sexual symbols hidden in the seemingly conventional scenes depicted in reliefs and paintings.

For example, monkeys are frequently portrayed under the chairs of seated figures. The ancient Egyptians considered monkeys to symbolically represent sexual activity. Another example is the golden panel from Tutankhamen's tomb showing the King shooting an arrow over the head of his wife. But the word for "arrow" is the same word used for "to ejaculate" so this innocent-looking depiction may well contain a reference to sexual intercourse. Again, there is much disagreement among Egyptologists as to the correct interpretation of these (and other) portrayals.

However, the everyday workmen were not so stilted. The findings at Deir-al Medina are particularly revealing. Drawings exist that portray various scenes of sexual intercourse. What we would call pornography shows up in the workmen's village. There is even one scene that appears to be children assisting their parents in making love!

TOMB ROBBERS

Tomb robbing was well organized even in ancient times. Corrupt priests and officials aided and abetted this activity. The Valley of the Kings was a prime target. This arid canyon was the burial place of kings from the sixteenth century BC until the twelfth century BC. Until the eleventh century BC the tombs were well protected and large scale looting did not occur. This was a period of relative stability and strong government. Then the pharaohs became weaker and the custodians of the tombs became lax in their duties. A wave of looting began and by about the tenth century BC most of the tombs had been plundered.

Records exist of a major law case concerning tomb robbing which occurred sometime between 1126 BC and 1108 BC. This involved dozens of tomb robbers but there is no record of their punishment (if any). At one time the dedicated priests and officials moved the royal mummies from one tomb to another in an effort to foil the thieves. In some cases this worked.

The tomb robbers in the Valley of the Kings and at many other sites were primarily after treasure. There was much gold in ancient Egypt and the royal tombs were a treasure trove.

But there were other depredations over the centuries. Many pharaohs ordered the defacing of statues, reliefs, and paintings of their predecessors. Stones were ripped from the pyramids to build many of the buildings in Cairo. As tourism grew in importance different items became lucrative to steal because tourists bought them. These items included small statues, papyri, mummies, and many other artifacts.

Egypt has been plundered for millennia. The story goes that French soldiers in Napoleon's army used the Sphinx for target practice. (This story may well be a myth.) Some of the destruction was the result of natural causes. Earthquakes and floods took their toll. The early archeologists were little more than treasure hunters. But it is important to understand that these men were sincere in their desire to spread knowledge about Egypt throughout the world. Also the science of archeology has only relatively recently come to the view that preservation of the artifacts of ancient civilizations in their original settings is important.

The artifacts of ancient Egypt are scattered all over the world. Many are in museums but some are in private collections. The world's longest-lasting civilization may also be the most widespread (at least as far as its relics are concerned). On a more hopeful note, the government of modern Egypt has, for about a hundred years, taken steps to protect the treasures that are left. It is now a serious crime to remove from the country any artifact of ancient Egypt.

It is not fair to characterize modern Egypt as having lost its entire spectacular works of art and architecture. Ancient Egypt was a wealthy and long-lasting civilization that produced an amazing amount of magnificent things. Plenty remains in Egypt, some yet to be discovered. Dr Zahi Hawass, the Secretary General of Egypt's Supreme Council on Antiquities and, perhaps, the most outstanding Egyptologist in the world, has said that seventy percent of what remains of ancient Egypt lies under the sands of present-day Egypt.

Perhaps the first tourist to write about Egypt was Herodotus, a Greek historian. He visited in about 460 – 455 BC. By his time Egypt was in Persian hands. Herodotus, his histories show, was a rather optimistic and gullible individual. He obviously was fascinated by Egypt and believed almost everything he was told. Despite his naiveté he recorded many things accurately. At the same time later writers repeated the tall tales he wrote down and thus much misinformation was passed down over the centuries.

It has been said that it would have been better for Egyptology if he had never existed!

One of the first tourists/archeologists was a remarkable individual named Giovanni Belzoni. Although born in Italy, he became something of a celebrity in England. But his celebrity was not due to his erudition, but rather to his theatrical performances as a weightlifter. To call him a "circus strongman" would not be too far off. He was about 6 ft 6 in (1.98 m) tall, incredibly strong, and became known as "the Great Belzoni." One of his acts consisted of his shouldering a heavy iron frame weighing 127 lbs (58 k), which was fitted with ledges. Then twelve people would get on these ledges and Belzoni would stroll around the stage carrying this tremendous load.

He performed in England for some eight years including in his act some tricks and what were called hydraulic displays. During this time Belzoni acquired knowledge of the use of levers and rollers and also of balancing techniques. This knowledge was to prove useful later on.

Belzoni's theatrical performances took him to various locations in Europe until, in 1815, he found himself in Malta. He met there a representative of the Egyptian government and told him of his scheme for introducing a new type of waterwheel that would revolutionize the Egyptian economy. He and his wife were transported to Cairo where he was to demonstrate his waterwheel. They arrived during an epidemic of the plague.

Changing their plans, the couple took a trip up the Nile, visiting the Giza Pyramids and Sakkara. After much difficulty Belzoni was able to construct and demonstrate his waterwheel. At first the demonstration went well, but then the waterwheel went out of control and broke the leg of Belzoni's young manservant. This doomed the device and Belzoni proceeded to hook up with Henry Salt, the new British consul general. Salt had orders from London to obtain as many artifacts from Egypt as possible.

Belzoni was a godsend for Salt and his plans. Salt hired Belzoni to retrieve the huge head of Memnon from the mortuary temple of Ramses II at Thebes. Previous antiquarians had known of the head and Napoleon's soldiers had even tried unsuccessfully to remove it.

Belzoni threw himself into the project and, despite many obstacles, succeeded by virtue of his knowledge of levers and rollers. The colossal head has resided in the British Museum ever since. After retrieving the head the strongman then proceeded to explore and collect a great many other artifacts. He also cleared the sand from the huge monument at Abu Simbel, discovered the tomb of Seti I, and explored many other tombs and monuments.

Although not scientifically trained, Belzoni had acquired the necessary skills to succeed where even an army had failed. His height and obvious strength helped, along with his Italian shrewdness in bargaining and his hard work. Belzoni probably uncovered more of ancient Egypt than any other single individual.

Belzoni was hampered not only by uncooperative officials but also by competitors chasing after the same artifacts that he was collecting. That he accomplished so much is truly extraordinary.

Following Belzoni there began to be a reaction to the plundering of Egypt. For example, in 1817 a French traveler bemoaned the looting that Belzoni and others were doing. However, this did not prevent the Frenchman from acquiring a well-preserved female mummy. He also advocated for an Egyptian national museum, but one did not come about until 1835.

Despite the reservations of a few, the looting of Egyptian antiquities continued at a frantic pace for at least the next twenty years. Champollion, the decipherer of the hieroglyphics, played a key role in persuading Muhammed Ali, the ruler of Egypt, to stop the exporting of antiquities of ancient Egypt. An important ordinance was then passed that banned the exporting of antiquities and the use of ancient Egyptian material in construction. The ordinance also established the first antiquities museum. The ban on the exporting of antiquities proved to be unenforceable but the Egyptians were at least trying to preserve their heritage.

It was around this time that scientists began coming to Egypt to study the ancient civilization, not simply to plunder it. They were the early archeologists and Egyptologists. At the same time the looting continued but it became more clandestine. This pattern of the illegal collection and exportation of artifacts continues, but modern law enforcement makes the reprehensible trade more and more difficult.

Perhaps the most famous of the early archeologists is Howard Carter. This Englishman was an excellent artist from a poor background. His talent was recognized early on, and at age eighteen he was sent to Egypt to record some of the marvelous paintings. He found himself surrounded by gentlemen scholars, yet fared well by virtue of his talent.

In 1899, when he was twenty-six years old, he was appointed Chief Inspector of Antiquities for Upper Egypt. Among other places he worked in the Valley of the Kings, making some notable discoveries. Also he brought electric light for the first time to some of the tombs. But he had a prickly personality, little tolerance for tourists, and difficulty with authority figures.

After a dispute he resigned from the service, but after a couple of years he became associated with Lord Carnavon, a wealthy English aristocrat. Although Carter was a stubborn loner, he and Carnavon hit it off. Carter copied his patron's dress and mannerisms and even began smoking cigarettes in a long holder.

The two men collaborated on many archeological finds and eventually co-authored *Five Years' Exploration At Thebes*. Egyptologists praised the book and Carter became a prominent member of the local Egyptological community. The two men continued their work and, in 1915, Carter became convinced that the tomb of the pharaoh Tutankhamen lay undiscovered in the Valley of the Kings.

They searched for six years without success. Carnavon, the funder of the project, was concerned about the expense, but Carter persuaded him to pay for one more season of digging. Carter chose to investigate a small triangular area near the tomb of Ramses VI. There they indeed found the tomb of King Tutankhamen.

The finding of King Tut's tomb is one of the major stories of archeology. The tomb proved to be the outstanding discovery of ancient Egypt. Actually the discovery of the tomb was merely the beginning of a long and messy process of recovering, cataloging, and preserving the "wonderful things" found therein.

For ten long years Carter disputed with disgruntled journalists, argumentative Egyptian bureaucrats, and many others. He finally managed to clear out the tomb and preserve its many spectacular artifacts. Most of these, including the Golden Death Mask of Tutankhamen, are now in the Egyptian Antiquities Museum.

An exhausted Howard Carter returned to England in 1932 never to be an archeologist again.

PART II

BETWEEN ANCIENT
AND
MODERN

Seth
'Great of Strength'
God of Storms &
Chaotic Forces
Brother of Osiris

As T.S. Eliot wrote, "This is the way the world ends/Not with a bang but a whimper," it might be said that the world of the Egyptian pharaohs ended with a whimper. From about 1000 BC the authority of the pharaoh appears to have declined. The structures and artifacts that have been found are less sophisticated. The economy seemed to deteriorate. The Golden Age of pharaonic Egypt was past.

During this period there were invasions of armies from outside Egypt. Although some had occurred from time to time in earlier days these invasions now grew more successful. In 667 BC the Assyrian army sacked Thebes and Memphis, but later withdrew. Over a century later in 525 BC the Persians invaded and Egypt became part of the Persian Empire. This was essentially the beginning of foreign rule in Egypt. This "rule by foreigners" continued until 1952, nearly 2,500 years. Pharaohs still existed after the Persians came but Nubia had split off from Egypt, hurting Egypt's economy.

The Persians were basically absentee rulers and violently disliked by the Egyptians. There was at least one rebellion between the time that the Persians conquered Egypt and the point when they were finally driven out in 404 BC. In the next fifty years the Persians tried twice more to invade Egypt but were repulsed, the second time by Nektanebo II, the last Egyptian pharaoh.

In 343 BC a ruthless Persian general named Artaxerxes III invaded the country. Within a decade Alexander the Great swept into Egypt. The Egyptians welcomed Alexander's troops as they replaced the hated Persians. Alexander actually had himself crowned as Pharaoh but he died soon after.

Following some twenty years of inept and abusive rule, the Ptolemaic line was established. The Ptolemys ruled for some 300 years until they were overwhelmed by the Roman juggernaut. During the Ptolemaic Dynasty, Greek became the official language, and Greek ideas in art and religion influenced Egypt. The Ptolemys introduced Greek gods but they also cultivated Egyptian gods and ruled much like the pharaohs. They erected great cult temples including the one at Kom Ombo.

Rome grew increasingly influential in Egyptian affairs until, in 54 BC, Julius Caesar attacked Egypt and by 30 BC Egypt was a province of the Roman Empire. Cleopatra VII, the most famous queen of Egypt, was the last of the Ptolemys. The story of how she became Caesar's lover and bore him a child is well known. After Caesar's death she became Mark Anthony's lover until they both were defeated by Octavian (later known as Augustus), the new Roman Emperor. Mark Anthony and Cleopatra each committed suicide. Cleopatra evidently had been attempting to preserve her family's rule and Egyptian independence.

The Romans, like their predecessors, adopted many of the Egyptian cults. They built many monuments, one being the temple at Dendera. Christianity found a fertile field in Egypt during the first three centuries after Christ. St. Mark founded the Coptic Church in Egypt. The Romans grew increasingly wary of the Church until in 284 AD thousands of Coptic Christians were massacred. Within thirty years Christianity became the imperial religion of Rome, but this did not stop the persecution of the Copts. Roman leaders, now ruling from Byzantium, differed in their theology from the Copts.

Except for a brief period in 616 AD, the Byzantine rule continued until the advance of Islam in the seventh century. However, as in Roman times, Egypt was a relatively unimportant "bread basket" in a mighty empire. After the Islamic conquest, there followed several centuries of power struggles and changes in leadership.

Then in 1171 Saladin came to power. He is still a hero today in the Arab world. In Cairo, he built the Citadel and turned Cairo into a great center of learning. Although he ruled Egypt for twenty-four years, only eight of them were spent in the country. The rest of his reign he spent recapturing areas, such as Syria and Jerusalem, which had been taken during the Crusades. The Crusaders returning to Western Europe took with them considerable medical knowledge. At this period in history Arab science, particularly medicine, was far advanced beyond what was practiced in Western Europe.

After Saladin's death his relatives ruled Egypt until 1250. Then power was transferred to a Turkish group called Mamlukes. The word mamluke actually means "owned" as the soldiers of the Turks were slaves. The mamlukes controlled Egypt until 1517 and, although the populace did not rebel, there was little respect for their Turkish-speaking rulers.

From 1517 to 1789 the Mamlukes remained powerful figures but the country was actually part of the Ottoman Empire. The government was run by pashas, career bureaucrats trained in Istanbul. Economic decline left Egypt in a sorry state.

Then the French, under Napoleon, came and went in a few years. The Napoleonic incursion was notable primarily because of its emphasis on the scientific study of ancient Egypt and the popularity Egypt earned in the rest of the world.

After a power struggle following the expulsion of the French, Mohammed Ali came to supremacy. An officer in the Albanian Corps of the Ottoman forces, Ali was an absolute dictator. He is regarded as the founder of modern Egypt. Many factories, railways, and canals were built during his reign. Ali and his successors remained in control of Egypt until towards the end of the nineteenth century.

Then the British wormed their way in and retained virtual control until the revolution of 1952 finally brought Egypt under the rule of Egyptians. There is no doubt that the centuries (actually over two millennia) of rule by foreigners have had an effect on the collective psyche of Egyptians.

Seth
'Great of Strength'
God of Storms &
Chaotic Forces
Brother of Osiris

PART III

THE TOUR

Karima, our guide

The Tour Group

THE FLIGHT INTO EGYPT

While waiting for our flight in the JFK Airport in New York we were greeted by a representative of International Expeditions who verified our presence and offered to help us if we needed any help. Although this contact really was unnecessary it was gratifying to know that we were being looked after.

Leaving New York in the early evening we landed in Cairo at noon the next day. The flight was as comfortable as a flight can be. Both the meals and the service were satisfactory. The delay in getting our bags and going through customs was less than what we've experienced in a US international airport. Most of our group was on this flight and we had met several of them in the New York airport or on the airplane.

EgyptAir is a major international airline that has been in business for some seventy years. Operating more than 400 weekly flights from Cairo and several other Egyptian cities, it serves destinations in Asia, Europe, Africa, and North America.

The Cairo International Airport is a modern, well-designed facility. Constructed in 1963 and based on a previous airport, it has two large terminals, and a third is being constructed. Terminal Three is scheduled to open in July 2007. The airport is northeast of Cairo, approximately nine mi (fifteen km) from downtown. It serves some ten million passengers a year.

Cairo International Airport

We were greeted by our guide, Karima. Since I had read on EgyptAir's Website that it maintains a hospital at the airport, I asked Karima about it. She said it was only a small clinic, but she wondered if my inquiry meant that I needed to go to the hospital. I assured her that I did not.

The bus ride from the airport to our hotel in Cairo was through what appeared to be an affluent suburb called Heliopolis. There were many military installations on this route as well as several mosques

Two views of the Mena House Oberoi

and other sights that we will examine in some detail later. We arrived at our hotel, which is called the Mena House Oberoi.

The Mena House is a famous and historic hotel located quite close to the Pyramids of Giza. As a matter of fact we could see the Pyramids from the balcony of our room.

The hotel was built in 1885 near the site of a hunting lodge belonging to the Khedive (then monarch of Egypt). The hunting lodge had been constructed around 1869 at the time of the opening of the Suez Canal. The lodge was demolished sometime between 1950 and 1978. At the time of its construction, the Mena House was well outside of Cairo. In the ensuing years the city of Cairo has spread to include the hotel.

Numerous celebrities, including royalty, have stayed at the Mena House over the years. In addition, it served as a barracks for Australian troops during World War I. Towards the end of the war the Mena House was converted into a hospital. During the war a young Winston Churchill visited the Mena House for the first of many visits during his long life.

In 1943, the Mena House served as the headquarters of a summit conference involving Chiang Kai Shek, Roosevelt, and Churchill. It was at this conference that plans for the invasion of Europe were finalized and the decision made that Japan would be forced to give up occupied Chinese territory and unconditionally surrender to the Allies. During this conference some 500 anti-aircraft guns surrounded the Mena House. There was even an RAF observation post on top of the Great Pyramid!

In the early 70s the Indian-based Oberoi chain of luxury hotels purchased the hotel. The firm spent a great deal of money refurbishing the Mena House.

Years later, in 1979, the Mena House was chosen as the site for the Egypt-Israel talks. Menachem Begin stayed in Room 908, while President Carter occupied the Churchill Suite, and Anwar Sadat the Montgomery Suite.

More recently the World Conference of Egypt - ologists was held at the Mena House. This was in April of 2000, attended by some 1,500 members. The climax of the conference was a banquet at the foot of the Sphinx.

In the evening we attended the Sound and Light Show at the Pyramids. This was not on our agenda but Karima said we could attend if we liked. Of course our entire group ended up going. Part of the show included the Sphinx seeming to speak. The voice sounded to me like the voice of Winston Churchill!

The Sound and Light Show is presented in several different languages at various times. At least one of the scheduled presentations was in Arabic so I guess this show is not just for tourists.

As we were dining in the elegant coffee shop of the Mena House Oberoi we observed a gathering on the lawn of a number of people in business suits. This apparently was a sales meeting or conference of Intel representatives. Evidently this hotel does a considerable number of such gatherings as well as weddings.

EGYPTIAN ANTIQUITIES MUSEUM

Karima, our Egyptologist guide, held a briefing in the morning. At this meeting it was decided that the group would go to the Egyptian Antiquities Museum today rather than to Giza, as indicated in the schedule. Karima recommended this change because it was windy and chilly that day and it probably wouldn't be the next day.

The museum is located in downtown Cairo and as we drove around town we observed many unfinished buildings. Karima explained that the reason for this is that builders are not required to pay taxes on projects until they're finished. Thus, often buildings are left unfinished. The buildings are mostly apartments; some are occupied even when not completely finished.

On entering the museum we went through security twice. It was necessary to check our cameras at a booth outside the museum. My initial impression was of large crowds, both inside and in front of the museum. It is said that more than a million and a half tourists visit the museum annually, in addition to half a million Egyptians.

The huge museum is packed with very impressive exhibits from ancient Egypt. We spent three or four hours in the museum but we did not come close to seeing everything. Visiting the museum was an extraordinary experience. Karima illuminated several of the exhibits with her commentary and this certainly added to the visit.

The Egyptian Antiquities Museum contains the greatest treasure trove of the relics of ancient Egypt in the world.

The museum was opened in 1902. There had been various antiquities collections even before that but

The Egyptian Antiquities Museum

the opening of this museum brought them all together in one beautiful building. The most spectacular of its 120,000 exhibits are the artifacts from the tomb of King Tutankhamen including his famous gold death mask and sarcophagus. Also extraordinary is the mummy room, which contains mummies of eleven pharaohs and queens.

In the evening we went out for dinner at an Egyptian home. Since our 22-member group was too large for one home we split into two groups. Our sub-group went to the home of Alaa, a tour coordinator with the Touring Club of Egypt, who was helping Karima with the arrangements for our tour. This proved to be one of the highlights of the trip (at least for me).

There were four generations of the family present. They put out a spread of eight or ten different favorite Egyptian dishes. We selected our food buffet-style and then sat around in a circle talking with the family members. Among other pleasantries, the family had prepared a birthday cake for one of the members of our group. It was an enjoyable evening.

I was fortunate to be sitting next to the family patriarch who turned out to be a retired general in the Egyptian army. The General talked of his experiences both in the army and, later, as a contractor. He had retired from the army in 1982 and subsequently had worked as a contractor in several European countries, including Russia.

He also shared his opinion that Muslims and Christians get along very well in his country, and blamed the news media for exaggerating problems. Although he didn't speak in specifics, I assume he was referring to the recent riots in Alexandria, which had occurred after a Christian church had screened a DVD of a play that depicted a Christian converting to Islam and subsequently becoming disillusioned. Among other points the play said that Mohammed was not God's prophet.

In discussing Egyptian presidents, the General said that he thought that Anwar Sadat would be recognized in the future as one of the world's great leaders. Sadat was president from 1970 to 1981. This was a different opinion than that of our guide who had said that most Egyptians looked upon Nasser as their greatest president. Nasser was president from 1952 to 1970. Mubarak, the current president, has been in office since 1981. He is apparently not as charismatic as Nasser and Sadat were.

Regardless of the individual views it was gratifying to see that Egyptians are free to express their opinions and to criticize their government just as Americans do. (But I gather they'd better not criticize a religion.)

THE PYRAMIDS AND THE SPHINX AT GIZA

Just as Karima had predicted the sun was out and it was not windy the next day so we visited the Giza Plateau with its three large pyramids and the Sphinx as well as several smaller structures. Despite the fact that I had seen many pictures of the Giza pyramids, I was overwhelmed to actually be there. There are no words that adequately describe my feelings as I stood in front of the huge stone pyramids that were constructed approximately 4,500 years ago.

The Great Pyramid of Khufu

The group was offered the opportunity to climb through the narrow shaft that leads to an empty room within the Great Pyramid. Many of us accepted the challenge. Most of the way up the shaft is on boards with rungs fastened to them at intervals. I was reminded of the gangplanks leading down to docks on lakes. The ceiling was so low that it was necessary to crawl on all fours. Although I am mildly claustrophobic I was not bothered by the narrowness of the passage. However, I found the climb to be more exhausting than I had anticipated.

The entrance to the shaft in the Great Pyramid

The Great Pyramid of Khufu (also known as Cheops) was built first. Khufu's son Khafre (also known as Khephren) built his pyramid next, followed by Menkaure, Khafre's son. The three generations of pharaohs reigned between 2551 BC and 2472 BC.

These are the three main pyramids at Giza but not the only ones. Three smaller pyramids, called the Queens' Pyramids, stand in front of the Great Pyramid. There are also more, and even smaller, pyramids located near Menkaure's pyramid.

Although not the first pyramid to be constructed, the Great Pyramid at Giza is the largest, its construction is superior, and it is laid out along precise directional lines.

The latter point has led to various interpretations. Some think the air shaft within the pyramid points directly at the North Star and thus indicates that the early Egyptians worshipped the North Star. Another theory is that the air shafts were intended to allow the spirit of the dead pharaoh to ascend to the stars. An additional theory is that the Giza diagonal (the three main pyramids in a line) is inspired by the belt of stars in the constellation Orion, which may be seen as a symbol of Osiris, an Egyptian god. Other scholars have seen clues to hidden treasures.

Inside the Great Pyramid are passages, airshafts, and burial chambers. Originally, a 26 ft (8 m) wall surrounded the pyramid and its satellite structures. Its base length is 756 ft (230 m). The Great Pyramid was 481 ft (147 m) in height and was the tallest structure in the world for millennia. It remains the largest stone structure ever built. (It's now only

about 450 ft tall due to erosion over the centuries.)
It is made up of an estimated 2,300,000 blocks of
limestone and granite each weighing about 2.5 tons.
It compares to the Eiffel Tower 1063 ft (324 m) and
the Statue of Liberty 305 ft (93 m). The Washington
Monument is 555 ft (169 m) while Kukulcan's Pyramid
at Chitzen Itza in Mexico is only 75 ft (23 m.)

Although it was believed for many years that slaves
built the pyramids, we now know that they were built
by proud and willing workers who were motivated by
a desire to serve their pharaoh.

Over the years there has been a great deal of
speculation as to how the Great Pyramid was built.
A people who had no wheels, and no compasses
built it and yet it was — and is — an engineering
and architectural marvel. They were indeed skilled
in mathematics, engineering, and science. They
developed a calendar based on astronomical
observations. They knew the principles of the lever,
the inclined ramp, and used rollers. They used
quartzite as a whetstone to sharpen their tools. They
had many tools, including saws, hammers, chisels,
and drills mostly made of copper. Native wood was
not very good so they imported better lumber.
Egyptian carpenters even applied techniques for
joining that are still used by carpenters today.
They constructed boats and furniture among other
things.

During Khufu's reign, the population of Egypt was between one million and two million. Among them were craftsmen, laborers, farmers, and others who participated in this great project. The building of the Great Pyramid was an important national project. Think of the Apollo Space Project in the United States that put a man on the moon. They were both commitments by great nations that reached for the stars.

The blocks of limestone used in its construction were quarried nearby on the Giza Plateau. The site for the pyramid was first graded and then a foundation platform was created. It was leveled and then tunnels were dug. One of the inclined tunnels (known today as the Descending Corridor) was dug some 100 ft (30 m) below the surface ending in the Lower Chamber, which was cut out of bedrock. A horizontal tunnel then extended from the Lower Chamber for some 50 ft (16 m).

After the tunnels were dug the stones that formed the pyramid itself began to be put in place. Three kinds of stones were used in the construction of the Great Pyramid. The core blocks were of Giza limestone, the inner layer of backing stone, and, finally, the outer layer of white Turah limestone. Granite beams were also used. Some of the blocks of stone were irregular so voids were filled with sand and debris. The pyramid was built in steps, with each step leveled after it was finished.

The heavy stones were pulled up the constructed ramps by dozens of men while the blocks were on logs serving as rollers. Remember, the ancient Egyptians did not have wheels. Probably some of the larger stones were simply skidded up the ramp with some kind of lubricant spread underneath.

The designer of the Great Pyramid and the supervisor of its construction was a man named Hemiunu. He was a cousin of Khufu as well as his vizier (a high-ranking government officer). Little is known about him but he must have been very competent.

Thousands of workers built the Great Pyramid, many of them highly skilled craftsmen. They were paid well and fed well. Their families were with them in the villages provided for them. In addition to the stonecutters, stonemasons, carpenters, toolmakers, and perhaps other trades there were also overseers, administrators, and draftsmen who joined the workforce.

The men were motivated not only by their pay (after all, a job is a job) but also by their desire to serve their pharaoh, the god-king. Sure, they were paid for their work, but they also had a motivating goal.

Although not the first pyramid to be built in ancient Egypt, the Great Pyramid was the largest and was once considered one of the Seven Wonders of the World. It is the only one of those seven still in existence.

We know that the pyramid was built as the tomb of the pharaoh Khufu — but why did it take the shape that it did and why is it so big? One theory is that it reproduced the mound that came out of the ground at the beginning of time. According to Egyptian belief of that period, this mound was where the sun god stood and from there brought all the other gods and goddesses into existence.

Another theory is that the pyramid served as a staircase to heaven for the soul of the deceased pharaoh. An ancient inscription in the pyramid reads, "A staircase to heaven is laid for him [pharaoh] so that he may mount up to heaven thereby." The Pyramid was certainly a symbol of the pharaoh's power and importance. The angles of the pyramid may represent the sun's rays on their descending path to earth. The many opinions about the purpose of the pyramids is evidence of just how much is not known about ancient Egypt.

Discoveries continue to be made that shed light on facts about ancient Egypt. Although the three pyramids and the Sphinx are what most people think of as the Giza structures there are actually two groupings of monuments. The larger grouping consists of the three pyramids, the Sphinx, attendant temples and outbuildings, and the private mastabas of the nobility.

The second grouping, separated from the other by a *wadi* (a usually dry water course) is made up of a number of private tombs of citizens of various types. Not quite a potter's field but definitely indicating a class consciousness in ancient Egypt.

The Giza Plateau has been a necropolis (cemetery) almost since the beginning of pharaonic Egypt, hundreds of years before the pyramids were built. Khufu, in building his complex at Giza, had to destroy many of the old tombs.

After experiencing the inside of the Great Pyramid of Khufu we viewed Khafre's Pyramid. Khafre was the son of Khufu. Khafre's Pyramid is not quite as tall as Khufu's but it is on slightly higher ground and thus appears taller. I'm sure this was done on purpose to out-do his father. (After all, don't all men want to exceed their father's accomplishments?)

The top of Khafre's Pyramid

Another attention-getting feature of Khafre's Pyramid is that it is the only pyramid that still retains some of the white limestone covering that originally adorned all three pyramids. The three white pyramids shining in the blazing Egyptian sun must have made even more of an astounding spectacle than they do today.

Khafre's is the best preserved of the three large pyramids at Giza. Khafre was not the direct successor to his father, Khufu. In between was Djedefre, another son of Khufu's. Djedefre oversaw his father's burial and then served as pharaoh for eight years before he was succeeded by Khafre.

The third pyramid is that of Menkaure, the son of Khafre and the grandson of Khufu. He built a conspicuously smaller pyramid. (I guess he wasn't trying to compete with his predecessors!)

This is the most unusual of the three Pyramids of Giza. The upper portions are brick rather than limestone. The lower portions have casing stones of red granite. Some believe that the reason for the bricks is that Menkaure died before his pyramid was completed and it was finished hastily for his burial. Menkaure's Pyramid was the last large pyramid built in ancient Egypt.

The Giza Pyramids were constructed around 2500 BC and for some 400 years were evidently respected. Then they were abandoned for several centuries during which time they were forceably opened and plundered. Then, in about 1500 BC, the kings once again began to show deep respect for the pyramids as monuments to their ancestors.

From about the sixth century BC, Greek travelers admired the Giza Pyramids and named them as one of the Seven Wonders of the Ancient World. Nevertheless, from about that time stones continued to be taken from the pyramids and used in buildings in Cairo. Thus many of the old buildings in Cairo contain stones from the pyramids. The vandalism ended in the nineteenth century, as a resurgence of national pride plus preservation efforts stopped it. If the vandalism had not occurred, the pyramids would probably look much as they did 4,500 years ago.

Following the pyramids we walked through the modern museum housing the Solar Boat. In May 1954, the director of the pyramids archaeological zone discovered a ditch just south of the Cheops Pyramid. When the limestone blocks covering the pit were removed a faint odor of cedarwood arose, and inside were pieces of an unassembled boat. Restorer Hagg Ahmed Yussef spent fourteen years putting the boat together.

The Solar Boat

The modern museum housing the Solar Boat is elegant with walkways above, under, and over the curved boat. The beautiful boat looks ready to be launched. The cedarwood has been well preserved by the Egyptian sand and the oars look as if rowers could use them today. The ropes are amazingly similar to those used currently to tie up large ships to piers. Also on display in the museum are some artifacts associated with the boat. All visitors to the museum must put slipcovers over their shoes, apparently to prevent sand from being tracked into the building.

Egyptologists are not certain of the purpose of the boats (which are found in other pyramids as well). This one may have been intended to enable the deceased pharoah to accompany the sun god on his daily journey across the heavens. Thus it is called a Solar Boat.

Perhaps the boat was used to carry the deceased pharaoh into the afterworld. A recent theory is that the boat may have actually been used to carry the pharoah's body across the Nile as part of the funeral ceremony. It was then dismantled and buried near the tomb of Khufu. But no one really knows. This is just one more "mystery of ancient Egypt." There is another boat still underground but not yet excavated. It has been located by X-ray.

The next stop on this breathtaking day was at the Great Sphinx. The Sphinx is, perhaps, the most famous site in Egypt. It is not nearly as high as the Great Pyramid but it is still impressive to see. The damage to the face is even worse than I had expected but that has little effect on its grandeur.

Called the Great Sphinx because there are other, smaller sphinxes in Egypt, it was carved out of solid rock at about the same time that the Great Pyramid was constructed. Parts of it have been repaired with cut blocks of stone. Several repairs have been made to the statue over the years — some resulting in more harm than good. The rock from which the Sphinx is made varies from a hard grey to a soft yellowish limestone. The head is carved of hard limestone of the same sort that was quarried for the pyramids. Most of the body is made of easily eroded limestone.

The Sphinx is 200 ft (60 m) in length and 65 ft (20 m) tall. The face of the Sphinx is 13 ft (4 m) wide and its eyes are 6 ft (2 m) high. Part of the *uraeus* (the sacred cobra), the nose, and the false beard are now missing. The figure is a hybrid creature, with the head of a human and the body of a lion. The head is adorned with a headdress, called a *nemes*, a sign of royalty.

The lion's body/human head hybridization is not unique among ancient Egyptian artifacts. Hybridization occurs many times in Egyptian art. The images of Thoth has an ibis head, Montu has a falcon head, and Hathor has the face of a human and the ears of a cow. Elsewhere in Egypt there are sphinxes with ram's heads.

The word *sphinx* is actually Greek; it is unclear why or when it became attached to this statue in the Egyptian desert. In Greek it means either "strangler" or "female monster." The sphinx in Greek mythology was noted for killing anyone who couldn't answer its riddle. Although it is not known whether the Sphinx had any religious significance when first carved, after a millennium or so it became a sacred monument. At one time it was considered an image of the sun god.

During the Greco-Roman period of Egypt the sphinx continued to be worshipped, probably by both the natives and the Greeks. In subsequent centuries it was, at least partly, buried in sand. The Sphinx's head emerging from the sand became an object to be feared and, even today, the locals know it as Abu'l Hol (Father of Terror).

The disfigurement of the face is a subject of controversy. Who did it? The common answer (and the one given by the local guides) is that it was the result of Napoleon's troops using it for target practice. But a French authority on the Sphinx reports three other theories. 1) The damage was caused by the vengefulness of the Mamlukes, who ruled Egypt in the fourteenth century. 2) Arab writers, from the tenth century on, told of its being damaged. 3) An archeologist examining the face of the Sphinx detected traces of destruction by tools that were in use from the third to the tenth centuries.

A stela (pillar of stone) is located between the forelegs of the lion's body. Thutmose IV placed it there in about 1400 BC. Its inscription tells the story of how it came to be. Thutmose was resting in the shade of the Sphinx during a hunting trip. (There were wild animals on the Giza Plateau in those days.) Speaking through the Sphinx, the solar god Horemakhet addressed Thutmose in a dream "as a father speaks to his son" and promised him that he would become king if he cleared the sand around the Sphinx. Thutmose cleared the sand and did indeed become king even though he was not the eldest son of his father, Amenhotep. (Perhaps this shows the power of Horemakhet!)

The deterioration of the Sphinx is widespread. Not only are the nose and false beard missing, but the lion's body is in bad shape. The wind and sand over the centuries have taken their toll. The smog in Cairo is not helping. Some experts speculate, though, that the fact the Sphinx was partly buried in sand for several centuries may actually have helped preserve it.

The face is a little off-kilter, the left eye is slightly higher than the right, the mouth is off-center, and the entire face is tilted back a little. Some see the Sphinx as having an inscrutable smile, somewhat similar to the Mona Lisa.

After viewing the Sphinx several members of our group went on camel rides. They seemed to enjoy the experience. One woman, though, began screaming as she rode, apparently not realizing how high a camel rider sits!

Driving along a canal that parallels the Nile we saw families living in mud huts much as they have done for thousands of years. I was puzzled by the news that we were going to Memphis, the capital of ancient Egypt, which no longer exists. How could we be visiting a place that isn't there?

MEMPHIS

The capital of Egypt from its foundation until around 1300 BC,. Memphis was located about twelve miles south of Cairo on the West Bank of the Nile. The name *Memphis* is the Greek deformation of the Egyptian name of an early pharaoh's pyramid, Min-Nefer.

Memphis was abandoned in the seventh century AD and later used as a source of stone for the surrounding settlements. Its ruins still existed in the twelfth century but thereafter it became just scattered stones. It is believed that Memphis was the largest city in the world from its foundation until around 2250 BC. Its population was over 30,000. Memphis is referred to as Moph or Noph in the Bible.

Entering the area that was once Memphis, we first went to Sakkara, which was the cemetery for the city, full of many tombs. We visited only one, which had a colonnade of forty columns called a hypostyle. A hypostyle is a building or space with a roof or ceiling that rests on columns. Here, the ceiling no longer exists.

The entrance to the hypostyle hall is flanked by a stone imitation of two doors swung open. The hall leads to an open courtyard that was once used for certain rituals performed by the kings of ancient Egypt.

The famous Step Pyramid dominates this site. We were not allowed to enter this pyramid or even to get close to it as it is considered unsafe by engineers who have examined it. The fact that these monuments are examined and determined to be safe or unsafe is comforting to know.

The Step Pyramid itself was the first pyramid built in Egypt, so it is said to be one of the oldest stone structures in the world. Although no other pyramids in Egypt were constructed in steps as is this one it apparently proved to succeeding pharaohs that a pyramid was a feasible construction.

Photo by Vladimir Pomortzeff

TEMPLE OF HATSHEPSUT

Photo by Ralph Hammelbacher

LUXOR

PYRAMIDS AT GIZA

CAIRO MOSQUE

A BUILDING IN THE LUXOR COMPLEX
(Note doorway near the top)

KOM OMBO

TUTANKHAMEN'S TOMB

KARNAK

Imhotep (2635–2595 BC) was the designer of the Step Pyramid. The Step Pyramid is over 200 ft (61 m) tall and consists of six steps, one on top of the other, with each step smaller than the one below it. The pyramid is built of limestone. The stone is not of the best quality, yet the Step Pyramid has endured for some 4,600 years.

A wall surrounds the pyramid and part of the complex. Only part of it still exists. The famed "pyramid texts" were found in one of the smaller tombs of the Sakkara complex. The pyramid texts were part of the Book of the Dead, which contains Egyptian spells and incantations, hymns and litanies, magical formulae and names, and words of power and prayers.

Nearby, in what are the remains of Memphis, is the so-called Alabaster Sphinx, which is actually made of calcite, not alabaster. It is much smaller than the Sphinx at Giza and its head is not the same. The Alabaster Sphinx has striations on its left side, unusual for Egyptian monuments.

The Alabaster Sphinx is 26 ft (8 m) long and 13 ft (4 m) tall. As with other ancient Egyptian monuments it has corroded over the centuries but it is still in better condition than the larger Great Sphinx. It was evidently carved between 1700 and 1400 BC. Some of the damage we see today occurred from the years it was lying on its side in water.

The Alabaster Sphinx

Close to the Alabaster Sphinx is a building enclosing a huge, partial statue that is said to be of Ramses II, one of the most prominent Egyptian pharaohs. As with the Solar Boat museum, this recumbent statue was difficult to photograph but here is the best Mary could do.

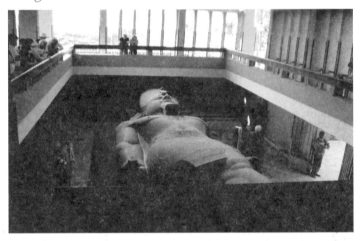

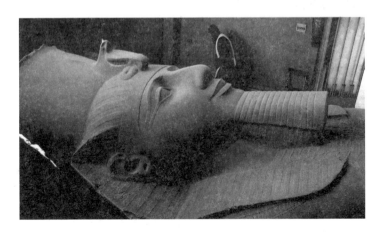

CAIRO AND LUXOR

We arose at 2:15 to catch the sixty-five-minute flight to Luxor. This ungodly hour is necessary because EgyptAir (the only airline in Egypt) needs the planes used in domestic flights for their international flights, which depart later in the day. Thus, all domestic flights fly early in the morning.

The Luxor International Airport, although smaller than the Cairo airport, is also a new and modern facility. Luxor itself is a city of about 600,000 people. Luxor was known as Thebes in Ancient Egypt.

The fabulous Temple of Luxor is very reminiscent of the Roman Forum in that there are many open spaces between the columns and statues.

An obelisk stands in front of the entrance to the Luxor Temple. Originally, there were two, but one was given to France and now stands in the Place de la Concorde in Paris.

At the base of the remaining obelisk there are four small statues of what look like monkeys. These seemed to me to be out of place here. One story is that the monkeys had erect phalluses until the Frenchmen cut them off.

Monkeys at the base of a Luxor obelisk

Just to the right and behind the obelisk (as you stand in front of it) are two colossal statues of the famous pharaoh, Ramses II. The sitting statues are on either side of an opening that leads to a colonnade on your right as you walk through. On your left is a building perhaps three stories high.

Oddly, up high on the wall of this building is a doorway. The guide explained that for centuries the sand had filled this temple to the level of this doorway and it had been used as an entryway to the mosque that was located there. Many of the Egyptian monuments had been partially or entirely buried under the desert's shifting sands. The Sphinx is another example of this.

Past the court containing the colonnade the visitor comes to another court which, in turn, is followed by a hypostyle hall. This hall has thirty-two columns. Beyond it is a Roman altar dedicated to the emperor Constantine before his conversion to Christianity.

There are many reliefs and statues throughout this extensive temple and some of the reliefs tell stories. One of the most interesting stories is to be found in a small room known as the Birth Room. The reliefs tell the story of the prediction of the birth, the pregnancy, and confinement of a Queen carrying a child, and then one god (Isis) presenting the child to another god (Amun). The baby born is Amenhotep III, pharaoh from c. 1391–1354 BC. There are more statues of Amenhotep III still existing (about 250) than any other pharaoh.

A fascinating fact about the Temple of Luxor is that it contains art from ancient Egypt, the Muslim religion, pre-Christian Rome, and Christianity.

The Temple of Luxor is, perhaps, the most impressive of the Egyptian temples. It is said that when Napoleon's army first sighted it in 1799, the troops spontaneously presented arms.

In the other direction from the seated statues is a long avenue of sphinxes. This avenue of human-headed sphinxes extends all the way (about three kilometers) to the huge complex at Karnak.

Avenue of the Sphinxes

The immense complex at Karnak was next on our itinerary. It is a vast open-air museum and one of the most impressive sites on our trip. There are dozens of structures of various kinds. The Great Hypostyle Hall was the highlight of our visit to Karnak. The Hall consists of 134 decorated columns many of which are holding up stone beams (also decorated).

As in most of the ancient Egyptian treasures, the amount of deterioration is extensive. However, the dramatic reliefs are mostly in good condition. Karnak is said to be the largest ancient religious site in the world. The Karnak site is distinctive in that it was built and used over a great length of time. Some thirty pharaohs built the various buildings and it reached a size and complexity not seen elsewhere.

In the evening we attended the Karnak Sound and Light Show. All agreed that it was more impressive than the show at Giza.

Crossing the Nile from east to west, we lunched at a very nice hotel and moved on to the Al Moudira. Although calling itself a hotel the Al Moudira is more like an oriental palace. Each room is on the ground floor and spread out among courtyards, fountains, and gardens. An amusing occurrence took place when an employee showing us to our room had difficulty finding it. Our room had the unique feature of the toilet and shower being in two widely separated rooms.

The Al Moudira is French-owned, a fact I learned when I asked to use the computer to check my e-mail. The laptop was in French and I was unable to figure out how to use it. The Al Moudira has a huge outdoor swimming pool and an excellent dining room. It is located out in the country and is far away from the hustle and bustle around Luxor and Karnak. There are beautiful flowers throughout the grounds. All in all, a delightful place to stay.

ABYDOS AND DENDERA

The next day we visited Abydos, which was a holy city to the ancient Egyptians. We traveled in a convoy of tour buses, apparently for security reasons. This was one of the security procedures so evident throughout Egypt. We all felt extremely safe.

It was about a three-hour bus ride to Abydos yet it was an interesting ride. Much of the ride was along a canal paralleling the Nile. Again, we saw people living much as they did thousands of years ago. Occasionally a satellite dish appeared on a mud hut. Paved roads, automobiles, and other signs of civilization showed up from time to time, particularly at bridges across the canal, adding to this jarring image.

Abydos is much less extensive a site than it once was. The magnificently carved Temple of Seti I is its most impressive monument. Some of the relief carvings retain their original colors. The quality of the relief carvings is outstanding, perhaps the best in Egypt.

As our group was wandering through this beautiful edifice we heard chanting coming from one of the rooms. The room apparently was the one known as the Isis Sanctuary. Observing from outside the room we saw three or four people facing a larger group of, perhaps, a dozen individuals. All were chanting and swaying their raised arms. It turns out these people were worshiping Isis.

The worshipers (both men and women) appeared to be Westerners. Someone who had talked to them reported that there was at least one Irish person and one American among them. I had no idea that anyone was still worshiping Isis.

In the same way that Muslims strive to visit Mecca at least once in their lifetime, the ancient Egyptians at one period wished to make a pilgrimage to Abydos, the cult center of the god Osiris. This holy city was once quite large containing several temples, necropolises, sacred lakes, and a town centered upon the Temple of Osiris.

Remaining today is the Temple of Seti I, the Temple of Ramses II (Seti's son), and the Osirion. The Osirion is also known as the Tomb of Osiris. Its huge red granite blocks and its stark and simple design are unusual for an Egyptian monument. The Osirion is located at a lower level and may once have been surrounded by water while the Temple of Ramses II is almost totally ruined. The Temple of Seti I, though, is one of the most magnificent in Egypt.

Egyptian history began at Abydos. The first kings of Egypt are buried here. Egyptian history began here in another sense as well. Late in the nineteenth century and in the early twentieth century, archaeologists uncovered the first evidence of Egypt's remote past. The ongoimg excavation of the royal cemetery at Abydos has added greatly to the knowledge of ancient Egypt. Before these excavations it was believed that the history of Egypt began with the Great Pyramid.

Among the archeological finds is the King's List located on a wall in the Gallery of Kings in the Temple of Seti 1. This list contains the names of seventy-six kings up to and including Seti himself. Another important, but puzzling, discovery is that of fourteen graves of boats. These were found in 1991. They were buried centuries before the Solar Boat found at Giza and are much more primitive. Nevertheless they are the earliest built (as distinct from dugout) vessels that have survived.

The Temple of Seti 1, like several other Egyptian monuments, has been reused first by the Romans and later by the Copts.

As I left the Temple of Seti and walked across the courtyard in front of it there were the ubiquitous vendor stands and — a short distance off to the right — the toilets. These rather primitive toilets are found at nearly every site. There is always an attendant out front who expects payment of one Egyptian pound (about seventeen cents US). For that most of them will give you a small piece of toilet paper.

As I waited while my wife was in the ladies' room, a young woman emerged and walked by the attendant without paying. I don't know whether she was refusing to pay or whether she simply didn't have an Egyptian pound. The attendant angrily called out after her.

Deciding to be a Good Samaritan, I walked over to the attendant and gave him a pound. He immediately relaxed and became very friendly. We told each other our names and he extolled at how beautiful a city was Abydos. His name was Achmed and he seemed very pleasant.

Of all the Egyptians we met, only once did we encounter any negative feelings toward Americans. That one time occurred when, at one of the sites, we ran into a group of elementary school kids who were apparently on a field trip. When they called out to ask where we were from and we answered "America" *one* child held up his fist with his thumb pointed down. In every other case where we identified ourselves the comment was "America Number One" or something similar.

After lunch we visited Dendera and, specifically, the Temple of Hathor. This temple is actually a Greco-Roman creation, built between 125 BC and 60 AD. It shows, perhaps better than any other site, the Romans' efforts to confer legitimacy on foreign rulers. In particular, the section of the temple that was built during the reign of Tiberius has reliefs depicting the Roman emperors, Tiberius and Claudius, making offerings to the Egyptian gods, Hathor and Horus.

One of the outstanding sights at Dendera is the astronomical ceiling in the Hypostyle Hall. Although not a sky chart, the ceiling is a symbolic representation of the heavenly bodies. Like most ancient civilizations, the Egyptians were very interested in astronomy.

Hathor as the goddess of the sky was probably the most important female figure in ancient Egypt (next to Isis). During the thousands of years that ancient Egypt existed she was known by many different appellations. Mother of Light and Mother of Love are two of them.

After admiring the famous ceiling we climbed a stairway to the rooftop from which we enjoyed the fantastic view of the surrounding countryside. We then returned to our oriental palace, Al Moudira.

LUXOR AND THE NILE

On this morning we crossed the Nile to the West Bank and viewed the famous Colossi of Memnon. These two huge statues, which originally flanked the entrance to Amenhotep III's mortuary temple, now stand alone in a field. Although badly damaged they still are very imposing.

The bad condition is the result of two causes: The Colossi of Memnon are constructed out of soft stone; not only that they also suffered an earthquake in the first century BC. They were built in the fourteenth century BC.

The Colossi of Memnon

Although the statues are of Amenhotep III, the ancient Greeks thought they represented King Memnon (a figure in Greek mythology). After the earthquake a crack ran through one of the statues, and when the heat of the early morning sun warmed the stone it was heard to give an eerie moan. This led the Greeks and Romans to make pilgrimages to "the Oracle of Memnon." The Romans eventually repaired the statue and unfortunately the moan disappeared.

At one time this temple complex was the largest in Egypt but little remains beside the two sixty-foot (eighteen meter) statues.

We made a short stop at the workmen's village (Deir El Medina). This served to give us some idea of how the workmen who built the pyramids and temples of ancient Egypt actually lived. We saw the remains of about seventy houses along a winding road.

The workmen who lived in this village actually constructed and decorated the tombs in the Valley of the Kings. The workers who built the Great Pyramid and the many other pyramids and temples lived centuries before the Valley of the Kings became the tombs of the pharaohs. From what is known of these earlier workmen their lives and customs were much the same.

Many artifacts were found at Deir El Medina including a large library of written documents, one of which is a description of a protest against the bosses who apparently had failed to pay the workers. (This may be the oldest recorded labor dispute in the world's history!)

The documents and murals describe many other aspects of the workmen's (and their families) daily lives. Deir El Medina is a rare treasure as the tombs and temples for which Egypt is famous contain very little information about everyday people in ancient times. Actually, the workers at Deir El Medina and other workers' villages may not have been commoners. They were skilled craftsmen and probably could be considered middle class.

Leaving Deir El Medina we walked through the village that has grown up in and around the Tombs of the Nobles. The village is a prime example of how modern-day Egyptians profit from the marketing of ancient Egypt. The village appears to be solely focused on showing off the Tombs of the Nobles.

The Tombs of the Nobles are tombs for the nobility, not royalty. The artwork, rather than representing the lives of the pharaohs, includes more imagery of life on earth and its continuation in the afterlife. There are very few carved reliefs here because of the softness of the stone.

In contrast to the royal tombs which were closed and sealed following the funeral, the nobles' tombs frequently served as shrines for the family. On occasion they were reused. A somewhat similar pattern exists today in the City of the Dead in Cairo.

The Valley of the Kings is in a very inaccessible location. Our tour bus took us as far as it could and we then boarded a tram that took us on into this desolate valley. It is surrounded by high hills of sandstone. The most striking aspect of the Valley of the Kings is how barren this rocky valley is. No trees, no grass, no bushes — no living thing is in the Valley of the Kings (except for tourists and flies).

A blind woman, a member of our tour group, mentioned to me that this was the only site that we had visited where she could hear no birds. We went inside several of the tombs. Some were decorated with exquisite wall paintings. It is remarkable how vivid the original colors still look.

A discovery was made a few weeks before our trip. Other than the discovery of the burial place of Ramses II's sons, this was the first find in the Valley of the Kings since Tutankhamen's tomb in 1922. The find was believed to be not a tomb but a *cachette* (a group of mummies). The site was still being excavated during our visit to the Valley of the Kings.

Subsequently the excavation revealed that it contained no mummies but was simply a storehouse for mummification material.

The Valley of the Kings burials occurred from approximately 1539 BC to 1075 BC or for about 500 years. The sixty-two tombs in the Valley of the Kings are not only for the pharaohs but also for some favorite nobles along with the wives and children of both nobles and pharaohs.

The most famous tomb is that of Tutankhamen. It is the most recent pharaonic tomb to be discovered, having been opened by Howard Carter in 1922. More importantly, it contained the most breathtakingly beautiful artifacts found in any Egyptian tomb. These artifacts, including the famous Golden Death Mask of King Tutankhamen, are now housed in the Egyptian Antiquities Museum in Cairo. It is ironic that Tutankhamen's tomb is so famous as the King himself was only a minor pharaoh.

About noon we boarded our Nile cruise ship and were directed to our stateroom. There are so many cruise ships on the Nile that some are tied up next to others rather than directly to the wharf. Thus we found it necessary to go through two other ships before getting to ours, the Ti-Yi. Ti-Yi was the wife of Amenhotep III and the mother of Akhenaten, two of Egypt's most famous pharaohs.

Our ship was very comfortable with all the amenities one could expect. The Nile cruise ships (there must be dozens) are all very similar.

In the evening we attended the Karnak Sound and Light Show. A security man took my wife's arm and hustled her through the crowds to an excellent seat. The seating was on the opposite side of the sacred lake from the presentation. The show was, in my opinion, the best of the three sound and light shows we viewed in Egypt. The first part of the sound presentation came even before we got to our seats. By the way, I would advise visitors to the sound and light shows to always carry a flashlight. This would be a good thing to have in the tombs and in some of the temples as well.

NILE VOYAGE

Before departing on our ship, several members of our group took the optional hot-air balloon ride over the Luxor/Karnak area.

Photo by Douglas Bartlett

The days on the Ti-Yi are undoubtedly the most pleasant of the trip. It is relaxing to watch the banks of the Nile as the ship cruises up the river. The ship itself is equipped with restaurant, bar (on the open upper deck), swimming pool, and two excellent shops (one for jewelry and one for dresses).

On a tour of the ship I visited the bridge. It was surprising how simple the controls are. As this ship (and others like it) cruise up and down the Nile it is not necessary for them to be able to maneuver very much. A member of our tour group was invited by the captain to push a button on the control panel. He did and the resulting horn blast startled us.

This morning we sailed for about five hours and docked at Esna. A number of small boats carrying vendors approached the ship and shouted to the passengers in an effort to sell their goods. If a passenger expressed an interest in a dress or whatever, the vendor would throw it up to the passenger to be examined and, perhaps, purchased.

In the afternoon, Karima, our guide, gave a very interesting lecture on both modern and ancient Egypt. She is obviously extremely knowledgeable about her subject. One of the most informative and refreshing aspects of Karima's presentations is the fact that she does not hesitate to inform us of the weaknesses of modern Egypt. Although appropriately proud of her country, she is frank about her country's problems.

Today we sailed up the Nile to Edfu. We rode horse-drawn carriages through the city of Edfu to the Temple of Horus. They say this is one of the best-preserved temples in Egypt. It is certainly impressive. Perhaps its best-known feature is the black granite statue of the falcon-headed Horus that is so often reproduced. The statue stands in front of the temple itself.

The huge pylon (decorative gateway) is behind the famous statue. It is the tallest pylon of all the temples of ancient Egypt. As we were walking up to the roof of the temple we passed a Nilometer. Although it looks like a stairway down to a lower level it is really a way to measure the flood level of the river Nile. The Nilometer was used by the priests of ancient Egypt to determine how much tax to levy on individual farmers. The level of the Nile determined how prosperous the farmer would be and thus how much tax he would have to pay.

The Temple of Horus was built fairly late in the pharaonic era, begun around 237 BC and finished about 57 BC.

The Temple of Horus was one place where the ever present vendors were kept within a specified area by the police. Following the visit we took the same carriage back through the city to the ship.

Leaving Edfu we sailed on to Kom Ombo. This is an unusual double temple which was constructed much later than most of the other temples in Egypt. It was built during the Ptolemaic and Roman periods. Dedicated to the crocodile god, Sobek, and the falcon god, Horus, it has two of nearly everything. It is one of the few Egyptian temples that is still close to the Nile. The river has changed its course many times throughout the millennia.

Among the interesting wall decorations are a panel showing medical instruments of ancient Egypt. Frankly, they didn't look much different from those used today! The temple at Kom Ombo was known as a place of healing. People came from all over Egypt to be healed here. Although no live crocodiles are around (they once were) there are two mummified crocodiles on display.

Taking a break from the tours of temples we plopped down in an outdoor café just down the hill from the temple. Karima treated us to tea and the men smoked the Egyptian waterpipes (*sheesha*). Our group was entertained by a group of musicians playing Egyptian instruments. *Fun!*

Tour members smoking sheeshas

Returning to the Ti-Yi, we prepared for the evening costume party following dinner. Most, but not all, of the group purchased galabeyas or ornate dresses to add to the festive air. The costume party was attended, not only by our group, but by the several other tour groups on board the Ti-Yi.

Costume party on board the Ti-Yi

We disembarked at the lovely city of Aswan. It has a tropical, African look and feel to it. Once on land we went back on the water in a small boat and visited the Island of Philae. The most prominent building on the island is the beautiful Temple of Isis. In ancient Egypt this was the center for the worship of Isis. This 4,000-year-old religion was Christianity's chief rival between the third and the fifth centuries.

The Temple of Isis, a magnificent example of ancient Egyptian architecture, was actually built over some 800 years during the Ptolemaic and Roman periods (about 300 BC to 500 AD). The temple was partially underwater after the first Aswan dam was built around the beginning of the twentieth century. Then when the second Aswan dam was built, UNESCO and several nations pooled their resources and had the temple moved from Philae to an island called Egilica.

Egilica Island was reshaped to resemble Philae Island and the temple was then moved stone by stone to its present location. This was a complicated project that took some nine years to complete.

Aswan, with a population of about 250,000, has what may be the most beautiful setting on the Nile of any Egyptian city. The islands in the river, combined with the many sailboats (*feluccas*) sailing lazily up and down the water seem to exemplify the slow, relaxed pace of life in Aswan.

About 3 PM we took a felucca ride. The felucca has existed virtually unchanged for thousands of years. The boat was large enough to handle our entire group. A narrow plank was used both as a gangplank and, from time to time, as a paddle or pole to push off from the pier.

Photo by Ralph Hammelbacher

The felucca sailed the river for a mile or so, enabling us to admire the several islands in this section of the Nile. The two main ones are Elephantine and Kitchener.

Elephantine Island is so named because its huge black rocks resemble a herd of elephants bathing in the river. It is located directly across the river from downtown Aswan. A large hotel is situated on it as well as a partially built hotel whose investors ran out of money before it could be completed.

Kitchener's Island is the site of a botanical garden, created by a British Governor.General named Kitchener.

Also viewed on the felucca ride was the Mausoleum of Aga Khan. Its pink granite is beautiful in its simplicity. Aga Khan III was the leader of a sect of the Shi'a Ismaili branch of Islam. The Shi'a sect is based principally in India but has followers all over the world. The Aga Khan apparently chose to live near Aswan as it was conducive to his health. He lived in the villa below where his mausoleum was built.

The armed security man who accompanied us on the bus also rode with us on the felucca. Security appeared to increase as we went farther south. One reason for this may be the Aswan International Airport, which is a military base as well as a civilian airport. The military, particularly the air force, is much in evidence here as they are tasked with protecting the Aswan High Dam. Near the airport are some bunkers that appear to be hangars for military jets.

It is said that should this dam be breached the resulting flood from Lake Nasser would drown ninety-five percent of the Egyptian people. The dam is so huge that it would seem to require a nuclear bomb to destroy it. During this visit to Aswan we visited the Aswan Low Dam built by the British from 1899 to 1902. This dam proved to be inadequate to control the Nile and so the Aswan High Dam was completed in 1970. The gigantic high dam is several miles south of the low dam. It created the huge Lake Nasser and changed the flow of the Nile. For thousands of years the Nile River flooded seasonally, enriching the soil of the Nile Valley, and thus providing the agricultural bounty that enabled ancient Egypt to be a great civilization. Thanks to Lake Nasser the Nile no longer floods and today fertilizer must be used on the crops of the Nile Valley. A positive fact is, half of the electricity used by Egypt comes from Lake Nasser. But the silt that used to enrich the soil of the Nile Valley is now settling to the bottom of Lake Nasser and eventually the lake will be filled in.

The silt from the Nile flooding, estimated at 4 million tons annually, not only enriched the farmland but also poured valuable nutrients into the Mediterranean that fed the sea life. This no longer occurs.

Another negative effect of the dam has been the apparent increase in the number of individuals infected with the parasitic disease schistosomiasis. This results from the stagnant water in the fields surrounding Lake Nasser.

Before leaving Aswan we visited the Unfinished Obelisk. This obelisk was never raised. It is more than twice the size (138 ft or 42 m) of any known obelisk ever raised. Evidently it was abandoned by the quarrymen after fractures appeared on its sides. It is still attached to bedrock.

ABU SIMBEL

We flew this morning from Aswan to Abu Simbel, a distance of about 180 mi (300 km). We saw very few people as we drove through the small town. This was Friday, the Muslim day of rest.

Once again, we enjoyed an outstanding place to sleep. The Seti Abu Simbel is spread out mostly on one floor, somewhat like the Al Moudira in Luxor. The hotel features an exceptional view of Lake Nasser.

On the shores of the huge Lake Nasser stands this great monument, Abu Simbel, perhaps the most unusual and majestic of all the temples of ancient Egypt. It is located in the heart of ancient Nubia and is almost on the border of present-day Sudan. It was built by Ramses II (c.1279–1213 BC) to demonstrate his power and his divine nature. Ramses II was arguably the greatest pharaoh in ancient Egypt and Abu Simbel has been called his greatest monument. He favored huge self-glorifying structures such as those at Karnak, Thebes (now known as Luxor), and elsewhere.

As with the Temple of Isis near Aswan these monuments were moved because their original site was flooded by the waters of Lake Nasser. There are two huge buildings at Abu Simbel. The most famous consists of four huge sitting statues of Ramses II on the front of one of the buildings. The building itself can be entered between the statues.

Abu Simbel

The other building is a monument to the wife of Ramses II, Nefertari, and is fronted by six statues. Again, one can enter the building between the center two statues.

Nefertari's monument

In the evening we returned to the site to attend another Sound and Light Show. In contrast to the other two sound and light shows we have been to in Egypt this one was performed in several languages at once. You could listen to the show in the language of your choice through the use of an earphone provided at your seat. Unfortunately, I couldn't get my earphone to work in English and thus missed much of the sound part of the show. However, the light show was very well done.

A word of advice to those attending this show. Be sure to insist that the person explaining the use of the earphone clarify the directions.

The four colossal statues of Ramses II are sixty-five feet (twenty meters) in height. Part of the statue to the left of the entrance has fallen, probably the result of an earthquake. The temple is aligned so that twice a year the rays of the sun illuminate the interior statues. This is an example of the astronomical sophistication of the ancient Egyptians.

The second temple at Abu Simbel was built by Ramses to honor both Hathor as the goddess of love and music and his wife, Nefertari, as the deified queen. The six standing colossal statues are more than 33 ft (10 m) high. There are two statues of Ramses and one of Nefertari dressed as Hathor on each side of the entrance.

Lake Nasser, which the temples of Abu Simbel look out over, is the largest man-made reservoir in the world. Or it may be the third largest depending on how it is measured. Lake Nasser is over 300 miles (500 km) long. Eighty-three percent of the total is in Egypt with the remainder in the country of Sudan. The Sudanese call it Lake Nubia.

In 1952, the government of Egypt made the decision to build a High Dam at Aswan, as I mentioned, a few miles upstream from the Low Dam that had been built by the British decades before. Two years later Egypt asked the World Bank for a loan to help pay for the construction. The United States offered to loan Egypt money but then withdrew its offer.

In 1956 Egypt nationalized the Suez Canal to help pay for the dam, causing the United Kingdom, France, and Israel to invade. The United States helped defuse that situation. The Soviet Union offered their assistance to help build the dam and Egypt accepted. The dam cost $1 billion to build. Construction began in 1960 and the dam was not completed until 1970.

There were major relocation projects as the water rose in Lake Nasser. Several archeological sites were dismantled and moved block by block to higher ground. Among those were Abu Simbel and the Temple of Isis on the Island of Philae.

The town of Wadi Halfa disappeared beneath the waters and a new town was built in its place. Many villages also disappeared and several hundred thousand people were forced to relocate.

In the 90s there were heavy rains on the upper reaches of the Nile. This resulted in record water levels in Lake Nasser which then required the Egyptian government to build another massive water distribution system called the New Valley. This was built to the west of Lake Nasser and created four new lakes. The area is so huge that it is visible from space.

BACK TO CAIRO

Today we flew from Abu Simbel back to Aswan. Since we had some five hours before our flight back to Cairo, most of our group went to the local *souk* (market.) Mary and I chose to walk the couple of blocks to the Nubian Museum, which was highly recommended. We couldn't get in, as museum admission is only granted with Egyptian money and we didn't have any. Karima had wisely advised us that we might not be able to get in without Egyptian money. *Always listen to your guide!*

The walk to and from the Nubian Museum was interesting despite our not being able to visit it. Our route took us past the Cathedral of the Coptic Church. Across from the church was a crowd of people waving palm fronds and holding pictures of an elderly man with a white beard. It turned out that the Patriarch of the Coptic Church was scheduled to visit the Cathedral later that day and these people were eagerly awaiting his arrival.

About nine percent of the Egyptian population is Christian Coptic. The Patriarch is to them what the Pope is to Roman Catholics. After our walk we sat down on a bench looking out over the Nile and fell into conversation with a man in a Western suit smoking a cigarette. Most Egyptian men wear the *galabeya*, a loose-fitting overgarment.

In the course of our conversation he revealed the fact that he was an advance security person for the Patriarch. He spoke of how the Patriarch was a much-loved figure by the Egyptian people — Muslims as well as Christians. (Our guide later validated this fact.) He referred to the Patriarch as "the man with the golden mouth."

Another interesting stop on this walk took place when we tried to enter the famous old Cataract Hotel. The Cataract Hotel is so named because the First Cataract on the Nile River is located near Aswan. This hotel is known as the place where Agatha Christie stayed when she was writing the book *Death on the Nile*. Also, the movie made fom the book was filmed here.

We were prohibited from entering the hotel because the Patriarch was going to stay there that night and security was already very tight (even though the Patriarch was not scheduled to arrive for several hours).

Luckily, a policeman allowed us to wander in the beautiful gardens. Naturally, I gave him a *baksheesh* as we exited the gardens. Baksheesh is an interesting concept. In this case it was simply a tip for a rendered service (since I didn't have any Egyptian money I gave him a US dollar bill). Sometimes it is more like a bribe and sometimes it is a request from a person Americans would call a beggar. It is viewed as sharing more than giving. The idea apparently comes from the Muslim belief that one should share what one has with others.

This concept is one example of the cultural differences that are so important for a traveler to appreciate. If an Egyptian person approaches you and asks for baksheesh, view it as a request to share in your good fortune rather than simply a beggar asking for a handout. Even though it's mainly a change in the way this is viewed it does seem to make a difference.

Flying on to Cairo we checked in to the luxurious Cairo Marriott Hotel. This hotel was built in 1869 as a palace for the French Empress Eugenie. It consists of two towers facing a lush garden with many tables and various attractions. The Cairo Marriott has all the amenities of a four-star hotel. Security was very much in evidence. Arriving taxicabs were required to open their trunks for inspection and everyone was ushered through two electronic metal detectors. There are many such detectors in different places in Egypt but some are very casually operated. Not so at the Marriott.

Our first visit that day was to the Citadel, one of Cairo's stellar attractions.

The Citadel is a medieval fortress which was built in 1176. Most of the rulers of Egypt lived here for seven centuries. Mohammed Ali, one of the last rulers to call the Citadel home, allegedly invited 470 important people to a day of feasting and then slaughtered them on their way to the banquet. This occurred (if it really did) in March 1811 and marked the end of the Mamluke rule.

Within the Citadel is the Mausoleum and Mosque of Mohammed Ali. After disposing of his enemies Mohammed Ali proceeded to tear down their buildings and construct his own. His mosque, also known as the Alabaster Mosque was built between 1824 and 1857. The vast interior space is dominated by the massive central dome. To the right as you enter is the marble tomb of Mohammed Ali. As in all mosques you must take off your shoes before entering. The main dome and four smaller ones at the corners are encircled by crystal chandeliers containing dozens of lamps. Karima took this opportunity to sit us down and give us a lecture on the beliefs and practices of Muslims.

We then went to another mosque, called the Sultan Hassan Mosque. This strikingly elegant building carries the inscription near the entrance "This is the most beautiful building in Islam." That doesn't seem to be an exaggeration.

From there we went to the famous Khan el-Khalili market and wound our way through this labyrinthine bazaar to the restaurant where we had lunch.

The restaurant is where the late Naguib Mahfouz wrote his novels. Mahfouz won the Nobel Prize for Literature in 1988. He is easily the most revered figure in Egyptian literature. Not surprisingly, the restaurant served a drink named after the Nobelist, an excellent non-alcoholic drink of tamarind and hibiscus.

The Khan el-Khalili market began in 1382. It is the largest market in Egypt and probably the largest in the Middle East. If you are a fan of markets the Khan (as it's called) will be a wonderful experience. Almost everything you can imagine is sold here.

The drive back to the hotel gave us our best (or should I say worst) experience with Cairo traffic. The drivers are (to put it mildly) insane. Vehicles do not stay in their lanes but seem to veer back and forth as the spirit moves them. Stoplights are few and far between. Pedestrians walk out into the street everywhere and seem to trust that the cars, trucks, and buses will not hit them.We are fortunate that we did not have to drive ourselves while in Cairo. It is amazing that people are not regularly killed, although according to a local English language newspaper, the traffic situation is of concern to Cairenes (as the local residents are called).

The Coptic area, the oldest part of Cairo, predates modern Cairo, which was established in the seventh century AD. There may have been a settlement here as early as the sixth century BC.

At one time this area was a Christian stronghold, with twenty churches within an area of one square mile. Only five remain. Jews migrated here after Jerusalem fell around 70 AD.

The Hanging Church is a Christian Coptic Church and a unique architectural creation. It is built across two towers. In the Hanging Church we observed a mass being conducted. The mass is different from that of most Christian churches, as the altar is out of sight behind a curtain. We noticed that the men and women were sitting on different sides of the church. The religious service continued even though there were tourists going through the building. There was also considerable remodeling being done.

Built in the seventh century on the site of a fourth century church the Hanging Church is the most famous Coptic church in Cairo. It has been remodeled several times. The only original section of the church is the section to the right of the sanctuary.

After the church we went down a medieval-looking street, observing the heavy wooden door that used to be closed at night. This was apparently to keep burglars from entering the street. This led us to the Ben Ezra Synagogue which (not surprisingly) was filled with Jewish symbols and artifacts. It is an attractive building.

The Ben Ezra Synagogue was built in the ninth century AD on the remains of a Coptic church that had been sold to Jews. The famous philosopher, Maimonides, worshipped here while living in Cairo. In the 1890s a hiding place was discovered in this synagogue which contained thousands of original documents from the Middle Ages. These included sacred books and legal scrolls.

Next we went to the Gayer-Anderson Museum, a dusty house filled with artifacts from all over the world. Many of the rooms are dedicated to a particular style or culture. One of the rooms is hidden and can only be entered by moving a cupboard to reveal the entry. The local guide said it is not known whether the room was ever used to hide anyone.

The Gayer-Anderson Museum was created in 1935 when the Egyptian government permitted a retired British officer to live in an old Arabian house. He had lived in Egypt for many years and was an avid collector. He assembled collections of domestic furniture, carpets, historic artifacts, and other objects representing the arts and crafts of Egypt. This spooky house was where part of the James Bond movie *The Spy Who Loved Me* was filmed.

We visited the crypt of the Holy Family. This is said to be the place where Jesus, Joseph, and Mary stayed when they fled to Egypt. I had thought that the word crypt meant a tomb, but it evidently means any underground room. The area had recently been flooded by a rising water table and much work is being done to improve the sewage distribution in this area.

The farewell dinner in the evening was held at a very elegant restaurant overlooking the Nile. Only Egyptian dishes were served and they were excellent. Egyptian dishes are tasty but not spicy.

This tour was a delightful experience that gave us many insights into an ancient and wonderful culture.

**Isis
'Great of Magic'
Sister-Wife
of Osiris**

PART IV

CAIRO AND MODERN EGYPT

Horus
'Lord of the Sky'
God of Kingship
Son of Osiris & Isis

Cairo is the largest city of both Africa and the Middle East. It has a population of over 16 million people, and it is estimated that 1,000 Egyptians a day move there. Founded in the seventh century AD, Cairo (originally called Fustat) was established by Islamic Arabs. The area on which Cairo is built has been important since ancient times in Egypt. For example, the relatively affluent suburb of Cairo known as Heliopolis was where the priests thousands of years ago worked out Egypt's elaborate system of beliefs.

What is known as ancient Egypt or pharaonic Egypt had long ceased to exist when the city of Cairo was established. There is a dispute among scholars as to when ancient Egypt ended. One school maintains that it was over in 667 BC when the Assyrians sacked Thebes and Memphis. Other scholars state that 525 BC was the culmination. That is the date when the Persians invaded and incorporated Egypt into the Persian Empire. A third school nominates 332 BC, when Alexander the Great entered Egypt, as the fateful date.

An exact date to the end of ancient Egypt is probably irrelevant. The pharaonic times simply petered out. From the reign of Ramses II, which ended in the thirteenth century BC, the power of the pharaohs steadily declined. Although there had been several foreign invasions over the millennia, the pharaohs and the nation now became progressively weakened and foreign invaders progressively stronger.

RELIGIONS OF CAIRO

Muslims

Customs — This book is not the place for a detailed description of the Muslim religion, but its impact on the daily life of Cairo is certainly relevant to this book. Most of the Muslims are affiliated with the Sunni branch of Islam.

One of the central tenets of the Muslim religion is the requirement that Muslims pray five times a day. Since the Muslim day begins at sunset, the prayers are said at the following times: at sunset, after dark, at dawn, noon, and in the afternoon. The call to prayers is broadcast five times a day from minarets all over the city — and there are thousands of minarets in Cairo. (This is not a quiet city.)

It is considered preferable for the faithful to go to a mosque to pray, but that is impossible for many. The person praying attempts to find a private place, but this is not always practical. Thus, it is not unusual to see a soldier, policeman, street vendor, or anyone else laying out a prayer rug and kneeling and bowing in prayer almost anywhere.

The religious beliefs of ninety percent of the Cairenes permeate the city to an extent not equaled anywhere in the West. There are carnival-like religious festivals called *moulids* that are held regularly. These are similar to the fairs celebrating saints held in many European cities.

Mosques — In the centuries that Cairo has been Islamic, many mosques have been built. The various features of these religious buildings have specific meanings. Minarets, for instance, are built with the primary purpose of providing a tall tower for the muezzin to call the faithful to prayer at appointed times. But their secondary purpose is to make visible the presence of Muslims in the community. They proclaim the presence of Islam.

Many mosques are domed. The dome may represent the tent of Mohammed. A *mihrab* is a niche in the mosque's wall which indicates the *qibla*, the direction of Mecca towards which all Muslims must pray. The *minbar* is the pulpit from which the sermon is delivered on Friday, the holy day. Many mosques have a fountain or wash basin for the faithful to wash their hands before prayers. All active mosques require all those entering (whether Muslim or not) to remove their shoes.

Art — Islamic art seldom depicts individuals. This is in keeping with Mohammed's preaching that people are not to be portrayed. Islamic art relies on geometry. Muslims believe that the harmony of the universe can only be experienced in pure geometrical form. Today's mathematics owes much to the Islamic civilization, which developed the Arabic numerals we use today and also invented algebra.

Many of the beautiful patterns found throughout the Islamic world have a deep spiritual meaning to Muslims. Some are no more than space fillers. Frequently, the patterns resemble stars or constellations. The geometric patterns are sometimes blended with Arabic calligraphy.

Christian Coptics

The Coptic Church, based almost entirely in Egypt, makes up about nine percent of the country's population. The Coptic faith is similar to the Eastern Orthodox Church. It had its beginnings when St. Mark came to Egypt around 45 AD. Mark was the first patriarch of the Coptic Church. From St. Mark there is an apostolic succession to the present-day Patriarch. This is similar to the Roman Catholic Church's papal succession from St. Peter.

The early Copts were persecuted as were other Christians, and they were even persecuted by the Romans after other Christians were accepted. But the stubborn Egyptians held on to the Coptic faith.

The split in the Christian faith between Roman Catholic, Byzantine or Orthodox, and Coptic stems from the early years after the life and death of Jesus Christ. One of the tenets of the Coptic faith is the belief that Christ was both human and divine in one nature. Roman Catholics and Eastern

Orthodox Christians believe that Christ had two natures — human and divine. There are many other differences between the Roman Catholic, Orthodox, and Coptic Churches, although they worship in similar ways.

Churches — Seven Coptic churches and two Coptic monasteries are crammed into a high-walled area in old Cairo. The most famous Coptic church is the Hanging Church.

Art — Coptic art is somewhat crude and conveys an almost childlike simplicity. Human figures are almost always portrayed in a head-on fashion. This is distinct from the ancient Egyptian practice of usually showing humans with the face in profile. In other ways Coptic art demonstrates a similarity to pharaonic art. For example, the ankh of the pharaohs is similar to the looped cross of the Copts. The pagan image of Isis suckling Horus is repeated in the Coptic image of Mary suckling Jesus. There are many other incidents of similarity between pharaonic Egypt and the later Copts. Some anthropologists think of the Copts as descendants of the ancient Egyptians.

Jews

There are probably only a few hundred Jews left in Cairo today but the city does have a significant Jewish history. The first mention of Egyptian Jews appears in Genesis. In Roman times there was a close-knit Jewish community in Egypt. The Jewish population grew to as much as 60,000 until the formation of Israel in 1948. By the time of the Six Day War (1967) there were only some 2,000 Jews in Egypt. Not surprisingly, there was a rash of anti-Semitic vandalism during this, and subsequent, Arab–Israeli wars.

Synagogues — The Ben Ezra Synagogue is a beautiful and peaceful location which serves as a reminder of a lost era and tradition. Ben Ezra is no longer an active synagogue, but there is a working synagogue in downtown Cairo, although it doesn't have much activity.

COLONIAL CAIRO

The major remaining reminder of the colonial days in Cairo is the Garden City section. Garden City is the area a little south of the center of downtown on the east side of the Nile. The British, who basically controlled Egypt from 1882 to 1952, built it. They wanted to create a bit of old England among the swaying palm trees. The ordered, tree-lined streets of Garden City certainly evoke London but nowadays they are something of an anomaly in the bustling, almost chaotic, city that is modern Cairo.

NASSER'S CAIRO

Colonel Gamal Abdel Nasser (1918–1970) was, perhaps, the dominant political figure not only in Egypt but also in the entire Arab world. His rise to the presidency of Egypt came about in the following manner:

After the crushing defeat of the 1948 war with Israel elections were held in Egypt. Nahas Pasha was elected Prime Minister. Then, in 1952, Nahas Pasha was forced to resign by King Farouk, who was head of state. King Farouk was little more than a puppet of the British, and a notorious playboy. He, in turn, was deposed by a group of nine army officers. The Free Officers (as they were called) chose General Naguib as Premier, but Nasser was the most prominent figure on the Revolutionary Command Council. In 1953 the monarchy was abolished. In 1954 Naguib was placed under house arrest accused of plotting to assassinate Nasser. In June of 1956 Nasser became president of Egypt.

In his fourteen-year presidency Nasser did a great deal to modernize and develop Egypt. Within months of becoming president, Nasser was the man who nationalized the Suez Canal, sparking a brief war. With the help of the Soviet Union, he constructed the massive Aswan High Dam. He oversaw the creation of an industrial base and developed health care, education, and agriculture. Basically a socialist,

Nasser expropriated the property of 4,000 of the wealthiest families. He also increased employment and education for women.

Not surprisingly for such a dynamic leader, he made some mistakes as well. He banned the radical Muslim Brotherhood in 1954 (even before he was president) and many of their members fled to Saudi Arabia. These men later influenced a new generation, which notably includes Osama bin Laden. A few years later Egypt joined in the formation with Syria of the United Arab Republic. The UAR collapsed in three years. Nasser's decisions led to the Six-Day War in 1967, which was won by Israel over Egypt, Syria, and Jordan. In that war the entire Egyptian Air Force was destroyed on the ground during a single attack.

For the city of Cairo, Nasser developed several landmarks. One was the Cairo Tower, some 570 feet tall. The story is told that this was built with three million dollars of American money. The CIA had intended this money to be used by Nasser to train his bodyguards. Nasser diverted this money into the construction of the Cairo Tower, which overlooks the city from an island in the Nile.

Following Nasser's death from a heart attack a million Egyptians marched in his funeral procession.

SADAT'S CAIRO

Anwar Sadat (1918–1981) had been Nasser's vice-president and became president upon Nasser's death. Sadat had spent time in a British jail as a result of his being implicated in a German spy ring during World War II.

As president he took Egypt in a very different direction from his predecessor. He ejected hundreds of Soviet agents and moved his country in a Western-leaning direction. He reduced the power of the government and encouraged private industry. He reversed the expropriations of the wealthy, returning the property that had been taken. Most famously, he flew to Israel and addressed the Knesset (the Israeli parliament). This latter action inflamed the Arab world and led to Sadat's assassination. But it also led to peace with Israel and the return of the Sinai peninsula to Egypt.

MUBARAK'S CAIRO

Hosni Mubarak (1929–) has been president since late 1981. He had been vice-president since 1975 and became president following the assassination of President Anwar Sadat. President Mubarak has been re-elected four times (1987, 1993, 1999 and 2005). A former Air Force pilot, he seems to be less charismatic than his two predecessors, Sadat and Nasser. Despite the fact that his picture appears on billboards and posters virtually everywhere in Egypt, Mubarak does not seem to be viewed as a popular president. He has survived at least six assassination attempts.

Mubarak has, during his presidency, seen the addition of two major new buildings added to downtown Cairo. A new Opera House was built to replace one that burned down in 1971. However, its thirty million-dollar cost was covered by the government of Japan. The other new structure is the Modern Art Museum. In addition, Cairo has seen a system of urban freeways, built between 1982 and 1988. A subway opened in the 1980s. Health services have improved and a vast sewage system has been constructed.

In Egypt the president is elected by popular vote for a six-year term. There are no limits to how many terms the president may serve. Prior to May 2005 the president was nominated by the People's Assembly and the nomination was validated by a popular referendum. However, a referendum approved a constitutional amendment that created a multicandidate popular vote.

This change was obviously approved by Mubarak (it probably wouldn't have happened otherwise). It is hypothesized that Mubarak was pressured both externally and internally to become more democratic. The external pressure probably came from the United States, which has contributed over fifty billion-dollars since 1975. The internal pressure may have come from the Muslim Brotherhood (or rather, from the fear of it).

Mubarak won the election in 2005 by eighty-nine percent of the vote. However, many irregularities were reported. Dr. Ayman Nour, his chief opponent in the election, was subsequently convicted of forging signatures and sentenced to five years in prison.

LITERATURE

Cairo's almost only claim to literary fame is the novelist Naguib Mahfouz. Recently deceased, he won the Nobel prize for Literature in 1988. He is still the only Arab winner.

HOUSING

This is one of the many serious problem areas confronting Cairo.

City of the Dead —This section of Cairo is a major slum. It consists of two cemeteries with many mausoleums. Between, and even in, the houses of the dead live hundreds of thousands of people. The practice of living among the dead apparently goes back to ancient Egypt and may have a connection to the belief in the afterlife.

Many families in the City of the Dead (the two cemeteries should really be called "Cities of the Dead") live directly above the graves of their ancestors. There are an estimated 300,000 residents in the City of the Dead. This is probably far more than the number of dead buried there.

MODERN EGYPT

Much has been accomplished during Mubarak's presidency but the remaining problems are huge and daunting. For instance, a third of the residents of Cairo are without running water. The underlying difficulty in resolving Cairo's problems is the rapid population growth. Cairo is one of the world's fastest growing cities.

Muslim Brotherhood — This group is the political party that is the main opposition to President Mubarak. It is in favor of returning Egypt to *sharia* (Islamic law). The Muslim Brotherhood has been technically illegal since 1954, but its existence is still tolerated. Members of the Muslim Brotherhood have been elected as independents to parliament. They hold 88 seats in the 454-seat National Assembly. Long accused of being a terrorist organization, the Brotherhood has now renounced violence.

HUMAN RIGHTS

A State of Emergency has existed in Egypt since 1954. It allows the government to imprison people indefinitely without trial. Mubarak continues to rule the country with an iron hand. Freedom of the press is limited, and the torture of imprisoned individuals is widely believed to occur.

BUSINESS AND THE ECONOMY

One mainstay of the economy results from the fact that Egypt has an outstanding educational system but high unemployment. As a result many Egyptians work in other countries as doctors, lawyers, and other professionals. The money they send back to Egypt is important to the economy.

Tourism — A $6.6 billion industry in Egypt, tourism is a major source of revenue and employment. Egypt received a record 8.1 million visitors in 2004 — and the government wants to double the number of visitors by the mid-2010s. Most visitors are Europeans, Israelis, or Gulf Arabs. North Americans are a relatively small percentage of the total number of visitors.

Manufacturing — The chief products manufactured in Egypt include sulfuric acid, paper and paperboard, cement, rubber tires and tubes, and televisions. Other industrial activities include the manufacture of iron and steel, the assembling of motor vehicles, and the refining of oil. The future for the production of natural gas seems bright.

Agriculture — Cotton is the largest agricultural product, but Egypt also produces yams, wool, and raw sugar. Other products include rice, corn, wheat, and fruit.

Government — In addition to the previously described presidency, there is a bicameral system consisting of the People's Assembly and the Advisory Council. The People's Assembly is made up of 454 members, (444 are elected, 10 are appointed by the president). The Advisory Council, serving only in a consultative role, has 264 members (176 elected, 88 appointed by the president).

There are, in addition, twenty-six administrative divisions called governorates. The legal system is based on a combination of English common law, Islamic law, and the Napoleonic codes. Judicial review is conducted by the Supreme Court. A Council of State oversees the validity of administrative decisions.

Communications — A reasonably modern telephone service exists along with Internet access and cellular phone service. There are a large number of radio and TV stations, some of which are government operated.

TRANSPORTATION

Air — There are eighty-eight airports in Egypt; seventy-two of them have paved runways. EgyptAir is government owned and is the only airline in the nation. Established in 1932, it is a modern and efficient carrier with flights to more than sixty-six destinations in Asia, Europe, Africa, and North America.

Rail — Government-owned Egypt Rail has 3,146 miles (5,063 km) of railroad tracks in Egypt. The principal line is through the Nile Valley as far south as Aswan. In prior years there were many accidents on the railroad but recently there has been improvement in equipment and safety.

Roads — Paved roads cover 31,000 miles (50,000 km) in Egypt.

Water — The Nile River is a major transportation avenue, although perhaps less important to the economy than it was in pharaonic times. Egypt has six ports and seventy-six ships in its merchant fleet.

MILITARY

In 2004 the percentage of Gross Domestic Product expended on the military is recorded as 3.4 percent. This compares with 4.6 percent for the United

States. Egypt has an army of 340,000, a navy, and an air force.

FOREIGN RELATIONS

Egypt, because of its large population and strategic location, is an important factor in both the Middle East and the greater Arab world.

Following Sadat's trip to Israel in 1977 the Arab world disassociated itself from Egypt. Egypt was kicked out of the Arab League and the League's headquarters was moved out of Cairo. Today that split has been healed and the Arab League's headquarters building is back in a prominent location in downtown Cairo.

Relations with the European Union are good and the EU is Egypt's largest trading partner. Diplomatic relations with Israel do technically exist but they are rather strained. When it comes to peacekeeping missions around the world, Egypt indeed contributes regularly.

Although Egypt strongly backed the US after September 11, 2001, it refused to send troops to Afghanistan or Iraq. This despite the fact that it had sent some 35,000 troops to the first Gulf War. President Mubarak walks a tightrope in his relations with the US even though the US gives more aid to Egypt than to any other country except Israel.

Egypt is a fascinating country, primarily because of its mysterious ancient civilization. This pharaonic civilization has produced some of the most remarkable monuments the world has ever seen. If you can possibly visit them — do so. You will never be the same.

ANNOTATED BIBLIOGRAPHY

Abas, Syed Jan and Amer Shaker Salmon.
    Symmetries of Islamic Geometrical Patterns.
    World Scientific: Singapore, 1995.

    A detailed discussion of the patterns in
    Islamic art.

Adkins, Lesley and Roy. *The Keys of Egypt.* New
    York: Harper Collins, 2000.

    The race to crack the Hieroglyph Code.

Augustin, Andreas. *The Mena House Treasury.* n.p.,
    n.d. Available at the Mena Oberoi Hotel.

    A history of this famous hotel.

Beattie, Andrew. *Cairo, A Cultural History.* New
    York: Oxford University Press, 2005.

    Not only a good history of Cairo but also
    a description of the Giza Plateau and
    Pyramids and Sphinx.

Bowman, Alan K. *Egypt after the Pharaohs*. Berkeley, California: The University of California Press, 1986.

A history of Egypt from Alexander (332 BC) to the Arab conquest (642 AD.)

Brodrick, M. & Morton, A.A. *A Concise Dictionary of Egyptian Archaeology*. London: Random House, 1996.

First published in 1902.

Budge, E.A. Wallis. *The Gods of the Egyptians*. 2 vols. New York: Dover Publications, 1969.

First published in 1904.

_____, Translator. *The Book of the Dead*. 10th pr. Secaucus, New Jersey: University Books, 1977.

A compilation of the spells and other writings of Ancient Egypt. First published in 1890.

Carpececi, Alberto Carlo. *Art and History of Egypt*.
Florence, Italy: Casa Editrice Bonechi, 2000.

Text with many excellent photos.

Casson, Lionel. *Travel in the Ancient World*.
Baltimore and London: The Johns Hopkins
University Press, 1994.

Contains useful information about travel in
Ancient Egypt.

Edwards, I.E.S. *The Pyramids of Egypt*. New York:
The Viking Press, 1972.

An excellent review of the pyramids.

Ettinghausen, Richard, Oleg Grabar, and Marilyn
Jenkins-Madina. *Islamic Art and Architecture,
650-1250*. New Haven: Yale University
Press, 2001.

Covers much more than just Egypt.

Fagan, Brian. *The Rape of the Nile*. 3rd ed. Boulder,
Colorado: Westview Press, 2004.

An account of the tomb robbing that has occurred in Egypt, including that done by archeologists.

Gauldie, Robin. *Globetrotter Travel Guide-Egypt*. London, England: New Holland Publishers, Ltd., 2002.

An excellent guide for travelers.

Gore, Rick. "Pharaohs of the Sun." *National Geographic*, April 2001, 34 – 57

An account of Akhenaten and his city, Amarna.

Grajetzki, Wolfram. *Burial Customs in Ancient Egypt*. London: Gerald Duckworth & Co., Ltd., 2003.

Funeral practices at different periods.

Hart, George. *Eyewitness Ancient Egypt*. London: DK Publishing Inc., 2004.

A picture book, primarily of artifacts.

Hawass, Zahi. *Mountains of the Pharaohs*. New York: Doubleday, 2006.

> An account of the building of the pyramids by Egypt's leading Egyptologist.

_____. "A Lost Tomb." *Horus, The Inflight Magazine of EgyptAir,* March/April 2006, 19-21.

> About the 2006 discovery in the Valley of the Kings.

Heikal, Mohamed. *The Sphinx and the Commisar*. New York: Harper & Row, 1978.

> An Egyptian Arab's description of Soviet-Egyptian relations from 1952 to 1975.

Ikram, Salima, *Death and Burial in Ancient Egypt*. n.p. Longman, 2003.

> A review of mummification and funeral practices.

Jenkins, Nancy. *The Boat Beneath the Pyramid*. New York: Holt, Rinehart and Winston, 1980.

A review of the Solar Boat, including its discovery, excavation, and re-assembly.

Johnson, Paul. *The Civilization of Ancient Egypt.* rev. ed. New York: HarperCollins, 1999. A large-format summary with beautiful illustrations.

Lehner, Mark, *The Complete Pyramids.* London: Thames & Hudson, 1997. A detailed description of the Egyptian pyramids. Profusely illustrated.

Lesko, Barbara S. *The Remarkable Women of Ancient Egypt.* Berkeley, California, B.C. Scribe Publications, 1978. An analysis of the role of women with emphasis on the fact that women had more rights in ancient Egypt than in America today.

Manley, Bill. *The Penguin Historical Atlas of Ancient Egypt.* London: Penguin Books, 1996.

A history of ancient Egypt with many maps.

_____, Editor. *The Seventy Great Mysteries of Ancient Egypt*. New York: Thames & Hudson, 2003.

An anthology of articles about some of the mysteries of ancient Egypt.

Marsot, Afaf Lufti Al-Sayyid. *A Short History of Modern Egypt*. Cambridge, England: Cambridge University Press, 1985.

Egypt under foreign rulers from 639 AD to 1954 AD as well as the history up to 1985.

Mertz, Barbara. *Red Land, Black Land*. New York: Dodd, Mead & Company, 1978.

A description of daily life in ancient Egypt.

Pemberton, Delia. *The Glories of Ancient Egypt – Treasures of the Pharaohs*. San Francisco: Chronicle Books, 2004.

A lavishly illustrated coffee-table book.

Ray, John. *Reflections of Osiris*. New York: Oxford
    University Press, 2002.

    Biographies of several pharaohs and other
    leaders of Ancient Egypt.

Raymond, André. *Cairo*. Translated by Willard
    Wood, Cambridge, Massachusetts, Harvard
    University Press, 2000.

    A scholarly history of the city of Cairo from
    its founding in 642 AD to 1986.

Richardson, Dan and Jacobs, Daniel. *The Rough
    Guide to Egypt*. New York: Rough Guides,
    2005.

    Another excellent travel guide.

Sellers, Jane B. *The Death of Gods in Ancient Egypt*,
    London: Penguin Books, 1992.

    About the gods and religion.

Smith, Craig B. *How the Great Pyramid was Built*.
    Washington: Smithsonian Books, 2004.

    An engineer/builder's analysis of the
    building of the pyramid. Excellent.

Sonbol, Amira El-Azhary. *The New Mamluks.* Syracuse, New York: Syracuse University Press, 2000.

A history of modern Egypt.

Tripp, Charles and Roger Owen, Editors. *Egypt Under Mubarak.* London and New York: Routledge, 1989.

A book of essays about modern conditions.

Tyldesley, Joyce. *The Private Lives of the Pharaohs.* New York: TV Books, 2000.

A prominent Egyptologist records virtually all that is known about the subject.

Vernus, Pascal and Jean Yoyotte. *The Book of the Pharaohs.* Translated by David Lorton, Ithaca and London: Cornell University Press, French Edition, 1996, English Edition, 2003.

A collective biography of the pharaohs including some additional terms.

Video Visits. *Egypt, Land of Ancient Wonders.* VHS, San Ramon, California and

London, England: International Video Network, 1993.

A 58-minute video that shows many of the sights of Egypt.

Weaver, Mary Anne. *A Portrait of Egypt*. New York: Farrar, Straus and Giroux, 1999.

Subtitled "A Journey Through the World of Militant Islam" this is a political history of the last few decades in Egypt and the Arab world emphasizing the inability of the government to control the violence.

Wilkinson. Toby A.H. *Early Dynastic Egypt*. London and NewYork: Routledge, 1999.

A scholarly review of politics and other aspects of Ancient Egypt.

_____. *Royal Annals of Ancient Egypt*. London and New York: Kegan Paul International, 2000.

An analysis of a collection of inscribed stone fragments known as the 'royal annals.'

Zivie-Coche, Christiane. *Sphinx: History of a Monument*. Translated by David Lorton, Ithaca and London: Cornell University Press, 2002.

A detailed description of the Sphinx as well as its history.

Index

A

Abu'l Hol 93
Abu Simbel 32, 55, 125, 126, 128, 129, 130
Abydos 20, 104, 105, 106, 108
Achmed 108
administrative divisions 153
administrators 84
Advisory Council. 153
Afghanistan 155
Africa 69, 140, 154
African 121
afterlife 21, 34, 35, 39, 40, 50, 112, 150
Aga Khan 123
agriculture 146, 153
Air 154
airports 154
air force 123, 148, 155
air shaft 81
Akhenaten 21, 22, 29, 30, 31, 44, 45, 115
Akhetaten 30
alabaster 97
Alabaster Mosque 133
Alabaster Sphinx 97, 98, 99
Albanian Corp 65
Alexander 21
Alexander the Great 63, 140
Alexandria, 78

algebra 142
Allies 73
altar 102
Al Moudira 104, 109, 125
Amarna period 21, 30, 44
Amazon 36
Amenhotep 94
Amenhotep III 102, 110, 115
Amenhotep IV, 22, 29
America 108
American(s) 79, 106, 108, 131
America Number One 108
Amun 30, 31, 102
Amun-R 34
ancestors 151
ankh 144
anthropologists 144
anti-Semitic vandalism 145
Apollo Space Project 83
apostolic succession 143
Arab 64, 93, 146, 148, 150, 155
Arab–Israeli 145
Arabian 136
Arabic 47, 74, 142, 143
Arab League 155
archeological 88, 107
archeological sites 129
archeologist(s) 25, 52, 54, 57, 59, 93
archeology 52, 58
architecture 25, 53, 121
army 155
art 42, 43, 44, 53, 142, 144
Artaxerxes III 63
artifacts 114, 136
artwork 112

ORDER FORM

INTERNATIONAL EXPEDITIONS

Name_____

Address_____

City/State/Zip_____

Phone(H)_____(W)_____

___ I want information about the Egypt tour.

___ I want information about other tours offered
by International Expeditions.

INTERNATIONAL EXPEDITIONS
One Environs Park
Helena, AL 35080

Phone: 800-633-4734

FAX: 205-428-1714

Web: http://www.internationalexpeditions.com

ORDER FORM

DIMI PRESS

Name_____

Address_____

City/State/Zip_____

Phone_____

Enclosed is my check for $19.45 ($15.95 for
EXPLORING EGYPT and $3.50 for shipping).

DIMI PRESS
3820 Oak Hollow Lane SE
Salem, OR 97302-4774

Phone: 503-364-7698
FAX: 503-364-9727
Email: dickbook@earthlink.net
Web: http://home.earthlink.net/~dickbook